The Microform Revolution

in Libraries

**FOUNDATIONS IN LIBRARY AND
INFORMATION SCIENCE, VOLUME 3**

Editor: Robert D. Stueart, Dean, *School of Library Science*
      Simmons College

FOUNDATIONS IN LIBRARY AND INFORMATION SCIENCE

A Series of Monographs, Texts and Treatises

Series Editor: Robert D. Stueart. *Dean, School of Library Science, Simmons College*

The Microform Revolution
in Libraries

by MICHAEL R. GABRIEL
Coordinator of Government Publications,
Microforms and Serials
Mankato State University Library

DOROTHY P. LADD
Associate Director for Technical
Services
Boston University Libraries

 JAI PRESS INC.

Greenwich, Connecticut

Library of Congress Cataloging in Publication Data

Gabriel, Michael R
  The microform revolution in libraries.

  (Foundations in library and information science; v. 3)
  Bibliography: p.
  Includes index.
  1. Microforms. I. Ladd, Dorothy P., joint author. II. Title. III. Series.
Z265.G33   025.17′9   76-5646
ISBN 0-89232-008-7

Z
265
G33

CONTENTS

Acknowledgements

The authors are indebted to many individuals who have given their aid and encouragement to the preparation of this volume. Although we are responsible for any errors of omission or commission, this book could not have been completed without the assistance of many librarians throughout the United States. Special recognition is due to the persons and organizations who granted permission to reprint illustrative material, especially the National Micrographics Association for allowing use of illustrations from *Introduction to Micrographics* and *Fundamentals of COM*; to Francis G. Spigai and *The Invisible Medium: The State of the Art of Microform and a Guide to the Literature*; and to Alan Veaner and the American Library Association's *The Evaluation of Micropublications*.

Chapter 1

Microphotography and Early Applications in Libraries

The bewildering variety of microform products and services that are available to industry and education today derive from the invention of John Dancer of Manchester, England, who in 1839 installed a microscope lens in a camera and created the first microphotograph.[1]

A renowned manufacturer of cameras, microscopes, and telescopes, Dancer treated microphotography as more of a curiosity than an integral part of his business, and he gave his handiwork away to friends and acquaintances as if the photographs were merely amusing novelties.

Other artisans in London experimented with microscopic photographs, which often took the form of individual portraits attached to rings and other jewelry. The invention soon traversed the Channel and Parisian jewelers and opticians added new twists by placing miniscule photographs in opera glass watch charms. One of the more successful entrepreneurs producing such novelties was Rene Dagron, who employed as many as one hundred and fifty workmen.[2] He and his competitors operated some thirty factories churning out microphotographic trinkets, and their success is probably in no small measure due to the variety of photographic art for which Paris is so justly famous.

The years passed uneventfully for Dagron until 1870, when microphotography was transformed overnight into a subject of national importance. When Napoleon III surrendered the French Army at Sedan in 1870, the Franco–Prussian War was only six weeks old. The Army of France lay down its arms, but the people of Paris mobilized and defiantly barricaded the city. For the ensuing five long months, Paris was surrounded by Prussian troops. All commerce and communications between the city and unoccupied France were cut off. The populace was reduced to near starvation and the pet population vanished, as did increasing numbers of rats whose satisfactory preparation taxed the culinary skills of Paris's finest chefs.

Under such conditions, the people were frantic for support and news from unoccupied France. Neither was possible with the Prussians controlling all access to the city. The Parisian Postal Service tried to reopen communications. First, they sent homing pigeons off with messages, but the number of dispatches they carried was woefully inadequate. Next balloons loaded with mail were set adrift. This proved highly successful, but unfortunately the traffic was one way. It was one thing to leave Paris and land in unoccupied France, but quite another to balloon toward Paris and set down safely in a target covering only six square miles. Scores of balloons left Paris during the siege; only five returned carrying mail and messages for the city's defenders.

Even messenger dogs were put into service to run the blockade. However, by this time conditions were so bad in the city that any stray dog was immediately snatched up for the stew pot and, despite the government's warning to watch for canine messengers, the experiment had to be abandoned because of the dogs' extremely high mortality rate.

Enter Rene Dagron. Since homing pigeons proved to be more successful than any other method of reopening communications, attention soon focused on a method of increasing the volume of dispatches. The Post Office Department approached Dagron and enlisted his photographic skills. In November 1870, Dagron departed Paris in a balloon loaded with his cameras, chemicals, and assistants. They overflew German lines and, after a series of episodes worthy of the Three Musketeers, finally arrived safely in Tours.

Using 35mm microfilm Dagron photographed letters and official dispatches, reducing them in size so that the films weighed only one twentieth of a gram. Yet each contained at least four thousand messages. The films were then inserted in goose quills and attached to the tail feathers of pigeons. Each bird could carry as many as eighty thousand messages across German lines. By the end of the war Dagron's "Pigeon Post" delivered more than two and one half million messages to the people of Paris.[3]

Dagron's services could not prevent the eventual capitulation of Paris in late 1871, but the microfilm copies of communication from unoccupied France did buoy the spirits of thousands of Parisians who otherwise would have been cut off from all contact with friends and family outside the city. The photographer returned to Paris and continued his work and further experimentation with microforms. He won several awards for his exhibits at the World's Fair and maintained an active business until his death in 1900.

Dagron's experiments with microfilm paved the way for applications in commerce and education. The medium also was particularly well adapted to the passing of clandestine communications, and soon microfilm became indispensable to the espionage craft. Dragon's greatest achievement, however, was in pioneering records management with microforms and proving that large volumes of information could be processed and easily transported on film. His "Pigeon Post" was so successful that it was modernized and reintroduced by the U.S. Army Air Corps during World War II as a means of transporting an ocean of mail across the Atlantic. The Army made microphotographs of G.I. letters in Europe, flew them to the United States, and restored them to original size at the point of destination. In this way one hundred and fifty thousand letters, that in original form filled thirty-seven mail bags weighing 2,575 pounds, could be filmed and shipped in only one bag weighing forty-five pounds.[4]

Six years after Dagron's death, Robert Goldschmidt and Paul Otlet published an article in the *Bulletin of the International Institute of Bibliography* in which the possibility of copying books on sheet or roll microfilm was explored. The authors suggested that books could successfully be copied on small sheets of film, a prototype of microfiche. They even specified the use of "Headers" or large print descriptive data (title, author, etc.) that could be read without magnification on the top of each card. They also described the attributes of roll microfilm, particularly in regard to economies of storage.[5]

Twenty years passed with scant attention to Goldschmidt and Otlet's ideas, and in 1925 they republished their 1906 paper emphasizing again the significant savings made possible by microforms. Shortly thereafter, George McCarthy filed a patent in the United States for a new system of microfilm processing and retrieval. He subsequently sold his ideas to the Eastman Kodak Company, which formed a new division—the Recordak Division—headed by McCarthy. McCarthy's invention made it possible to microfilm cancelled bank checks and viewing machines were designed for use in searching and reading documents. This process was marketed under the trade name Recordak, and it soon found wide acceptance in banks, insurance companies, and then libraries.

Although the development and acceptance of microforms occurred much faster in commerce than in education, the potential benefits to libraries were not entirely ignored. As described by Eugene Power of University Microfilms, the primary applications were: (1) a means of protecting books, manuscripts, and documents against loss and unnecessary use; (2) securing permanent copies of ephemeral material; (3) obtaining copies of material in distant depositories; (4) reducing the space occupied by a collection of materials in traditional formats; (5) original publications of scholarly and technical material; (6) republishing material in short supply or out of print.[6]

The League of Nations Committee of Library Experts investigated the suitability of microfilm for documentation in 1928, the same year in which the Recordak microfilm camera was introduced. With the subsequent development of the Leica camera, many individual scholars began microcopying manuscripts and archival material. Many American researchers made microcopies in Europe and then brought them back to their own libraries, so that by the early 1930s several research libraries including Harvard, Yale, and the Library of Congress were building microform collections and were accepting orders for film copies.

In 1935 the United States Government took the first step in what eventually became a massive microform program with the filming of some 300,000 pages of the hearings of the National Recovery Administration and the Agricultural Adjustment Agency. This project was conceived when several American libraries requested copies of the paper hearings.[7]

The joint financing by several libraries of the NRA and AAA hearings led to many cooperative projects aimed at acquisition of rare and expensive resources. In 1935 Eugene Power began filming English books printed prior to 1550—the beginning of the *Short Title Catalogue Series*. A short time later Power founded University Microfilms and initiated *Dissertation Abstracts* and the filming of doctoral dissertations, thereby assuring the firm a long and mutually profitable association with the library community.

In *The Scholar and the Future of the Research Library, a Problem and its Solution* published in 1944, Fremont Rider pointed out the exponential rate of growth in research libraries and argued that microforms were the most rational solution to the problems of storage for growing collections. Rider predicted that by the year 2040 the Yale University Library would own more than 200 million volumes taking up more than six thousand miles of shelving. The library's card catalog would occupy eight acres of floor space and a cataloging staff of more than six thousand would be required to process the more than twelve million volumes received annually.

Rider's answer to the danger of libraries transformed into Augean stables, was to produce 3 × 5 inch micro-opaque cards of each item owned by research libraries. The front of each card would contain cataloging information for the individual document fully reproduced on the reverse of the card, thus the entire library could be housed in a standard card catalog obviating the necessity for traditional book stacks. Items could be circulated simply by placing a call slip in the correct position of the catalog for any particular document. Or the patron could reproduce a copy of the card in a duplicator, leaving the original card for other users. Rider argued that savings in space with his program would approach 100 percent because book-stacks would be required for only a few reference books.[8]

Rider's ideas dropped like lead weights in bottomless wells of the library community. No library converted its holdings to micro-opaques. And when the Readex Microprint Corporation developed the 6 × 9 inch opaque Microprint card in 1950, attention focused on the production of esoteric research materials with secondary regard for the space saving qualities of the medium.[9]

The Microprint produced by Readex contained text printed

by offset on calendered paper at a reduction of 12–18 diameters. The smooth surface of calendered paper facilitated printing of the miniscule letters, and the low cost of production (opaques are the least expensive microform to produce, particularly in large editions) triggered many publishing endeavors, notably the *British Sessional Papers* and *Three Centuries of English and American Plays, 1500–1800.*

These initial projects by the country's first micropublishers were illustrative of the future direction microform publishing would take for the library market. The filming of rare and scattered information sources was widely acclaimed by scholars, for microforms—despite the unfamiliarity of the new medium and the inferior quality of early reading devices—facilitated transfer of information that was usually inaccessible in original formats. They also were clearly superior to some original formats, as with newspapers where film is vastly superior to bulky and deteriorating paper copies.

Resistance developed, however, as microforms intruded on the market traditionally held by publications widely available in paper. Although the costs to libraries of maintaining many information sources in microform are substantially lower than with paper (e.g., serials), the grudging acceptance of any revolutionary new technology is no less formidable in the library community than in society at large. Nor was acceptance aided by the confusing multiplicity of microforms, the generally low quality of reading devices, and the fact that library needs seemed secondary to manufacturers of microform systems who rapidly exploited the commercial and industrial markets.

Despite these obstacles, the generous funding of libraries during the 1950s and 1960s stimulated increasingly larger microform collections in all types of libraries, especially academic. By 1970, the member institutions of the Association of Research Libraries were reporting more than half a million microform units per library.[10] If the acquisition rates for microfilm, microfiche, and microcards were translated into page equivalents, these libraries each were adding more than 500 million pages of microform every year,[11] and the proportion of microforms to books in research libraries was approaching twenty-five percent.[12]

The continuing development of microform technology undoubtably will increase the ratio of microforms to books. The marriage of the computer and the microtext is revolutionizing information storage and retrieval. Today, Vannever Bush's 1945 vision of an ideal scholar's library—a desk sized carrel containing reproductions of all the papers and books of interest to any scholar—does not seem so preposterous.[13] *The New York Times* Information Bank combines a computer, printer, and microfiche duplicator with the capability to provide a researcher in Alaska with information on any subject imaginable from the files of *The Times* in New York City.

The next stage of evolution could be the "duplicating" or "desk top" library where most reference tools would remain in book form but other materials would be miniaturized. In this library no copy would ever be missing or in circulation, for copies would be duplicated and given or sold to users on demand. A microform master copy would remain in the library at all times for duplicating purposes, and users would build personal microform collections at lower cost than is now possible with printed copies. Low cost, portable microform readers could be loaned or leased by libraries, or patrons could purchase personal units.[14]

The "duplicating library" concept creates complex problems of copyright and equitable renumeration for authors and publishers. But the problem is scarcely insurmountable, and duplicating libraries may soon develop in logical progression from original publishing in microform and "packaged libraries." Collections of general and specialized materials offered in packages, such as ERIC, PCMI, Library of American Civilization, etc., gained wide acceptance, particularly in new libaries that needed to build learning resources and could do so at lower cost with microforms than with expensive and often unobtainable originals. Small and medium sized academic libraries frequently purchased such collections to support graduate research or to supplement existing collections. And research libraries are increasingly interested in converting from paper to microform. The enormous potential to achieve savings by duplicating microforms for users rather than circulating books, the increased accessibility (approaching one hundred percent) of materials that will be available when needed, the vast decentralization of cultural resources made possible by duplication of microforms enabling every city to have a library as rich as the New York Public—these are compelling reasons why microforms are and will continue to be an expanding galaxy in the library and educational universe.[15]

The opportunity for dynamic growth in the use of microforms exists in all of the library community, and especially in academe. Reading for pleasure undoubtably will continue to be the private domain of printed material for a long time to come. But motives other than pleasure dominate educational reading, and the relative inconvenience of utilizing microforms is preferable than doing without. Such a choice is now commonplace in many academic libraries whose economic condition has been steadily deteriorating during the decade of the seventies. Enormous potential for growth also exists with the tens of millions of students in elementary and secondary schools where innovative programs already have demonstrated the comparability, and in some cases superiority, of microforms vis à vis traditional learning and teaching materials.[16] The pervasive acceptance and acquisition of electronic media by our children is too widely felt to need restating here; it is merely one more nail in the coffin of Gutenberg technology. For, as Kleukens and Goebel predicted more than thirty years ago in, appropriately, Mainz, Germany, we have entered a third technological era in communications dominated by film and electronic media, and thus the chronicled history of microforms is but one page in an ongoing epoch.[17]

NOTES

1. Nanney, Thomas G. *Using Microfilm Effectively* (New York: Geyer-McAllister, 1968), p. 1.

2. Stevens, G.W. *Microphotography* (New York: John Wiley & Sons, 1968), p. 3.

3. Luther, Frank. *Microfilm: A History* (Annapolis: National Microfilm Association, 1950), p. 140

4. "Microscopic Mailbag," *Popular Science* (January 1953), pp. 100–101.

5. Hawkins, Reginald. *Production of Micro-Forms* (New Brunswick, N.J.: Rutgers University Press, 1960).

6. Power, Eugene B. "University Microfilms—A Microfilming Service for Scholars," *Journal of Documentation* 2 (1946–1947): 23–31.

7. Stevens, Rolland E. "Resources in Microform for the Research Library," *Microform Review* 1 (January 1972): 9.

8. Rider, Fremont. *The Scholar and the Future of the Research Library, a Problem and its Solution* (New York: Hadham Press, 1944).

9. Stevens, Rolland E. "The Microform Revolution," *Library Trends* 19(3) (January 1971): 379–95.

10. Association of Research Libraries, *Academic Library Statistics, 1969/70* (Washington, D.C.: ARL, 1970).

11. Spreitzer, Francis F. "Developments in Copying, Micrographics, and Graphic Communications, 1972," *Library Resources and Technical Services* 17 (Spring 1973): V151.

12. Reichmann, Felix. "Bibliographical Control of Microforms," *Microform Review* 1: (October 1972): 279.

13. Bush, Vannevar. "As We May Think," *Atlantic Monthly* 176 (July, 1945): 106–07.

14. Heilprin, L.B. "The Economics of on-Demand Copying," National Microfilm Association, *Proceedings*, Vol. 11 (Annapolis, Md., 1962), pp. 311–39.

15. Starr, Paul. "Transforming the Libraries from Paper to Microfiche," *Change* (November 1974), pp. 34–40.

16. Burchinal, Lee G. "Uses of Microfilm in Educational Institutions," *The Journal of Micrographics* 7(3) (January 1974): 107–112.

17. Kleukens, C. H. and Goebel, J. *Schrift, Letter, Microkopie* [Handwriting, Type, Microcopy] Mainzer Presse, 1940.

Chapter 2

Microformats and Associated Library Collections

The complex assortment of microforms in libraries is a reality that no amount of pleading for standardization is likely to change. If form follows function, as it ideally should, long runs of newspapers will continue to appear on roll microfilm, just as monographic collections increasingly will succumb to reproduction on microfiche. Intended use should dictate the choice between sheet or roll film, as well as the reduction ratio, contrast, and film type. The Recordak system was designed to film bank checks which do not require frequent retrieval. Substituting microfiche for the 16mm film on which checks are processed would only increase costs and complicate filming and retrieval of the records. Technical report literature appears almost exclusively on low reduction microfiche. These reports are monographic in nature and benefit from the unitization that fiche affords. Convenience of use would not be as great with film as it is with fiche. These are examples of how specific microforms were designed or evolved to meet specific needs. Further evolution should ideally follow the maxim that microforms should be designed to follow function and probable frequency of use.

Microformats can be conveniently categorized as either roll or flat mediums. Within the two forms there is a myriad assortment of frame sizes, orientations (internal formats) and reduction ratios. Roll films in standard 100 feet lengths at reduction ratios of 24.1 contain more than 3000 pages of material. Flat mediums (4 × 6 fiche, microcard) hold about 100 pages in medium reduction ratios (18–24×) and up to 6000 pages in ultra-high reduction ratos.

MICROFILM

Roll microfilm is usually 100 feet in length and 16mm or 35mm in width. In libraries, materials that are published in long runs (e.g., newspapers) frequently appear on microfilm. In recent years roll microfilm loaded in cartridges and cassettes has replaced some microfilm on reels because of the speed and ease of handling packaged film. Cartridges are self-threading containers. Unlike cassettes they have only one film core and must be rewound after using. Cassettes, on the other hand, can be removed from the viewer at any time with any frame remaining

Figure 1

roll microfilm

Microfilm—regardless of its ultimate format for storage - - is, in almost all cases, first produced as roll film on a reel. Roll film is the least expensive form in which microfilm can be produced and duplicated.

File integrity and security

In addition to its low cost, roll film offers other advantages. Among them:

File integrity—the ability to retrieve and reproduce a document without the chance of its being lost or misfiled after use.

File security—the use of microfilm to duplicate irreplaceable records as assurance against the loss or destruction of the originals.

Choice of format determined by user need

Documents may be recorded and reproduced on roll film in many formats and styles, depending on the nature of the material and how it is to be used. The standard roll film formats are shown on these two pages.

Some users require a microfilm system that can reproduce documents within a wide range of sizes—from large engineering drawings to a small file card. Some, like banks and law firms, need a system that can reproduce both front and back of a document (a cancelled check or a notarized deed) side by side. Some require capability for automated or computerized document retrieval. Whatever the requirement, there is a roll microfilm format to accommodate it.

Roll microfilm is available in reels, cartridges, and cassettes.

simplex, duo & duplex

These terms refer to the arrangement of the documents contained on the microfilm.

simplex format

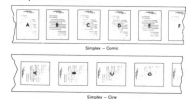

Simplex — Comic

Simplex — Cine

Film is run through the camera once, and a single row of images is photographed. Documents of various widths and lengths are accommodated. Image orientation can be *comic*, with information right reading from edge to edge of the film, or *cine*, with information right reading along the length of the film.

duplex format

Both the front and back of a document, both sides of a check for example, are photographed simultaneously side by side on the film, across the width.

in a reading position for future reference. Sixteen millimeter film is commonly used in cassettes and cartridges.

Cartridges and cassettes are normally used in motorized readers and, although more expensive, they clearly are superior to reel microfilm in many applications since they permit rapid and convenient searching and extracting of information.

Microfilm begins with the selection of a book or some other material to be photographed. Fine grained, high contrast film is used to make microfilm, and there are three types of photo-sensitive coatings routinely used on these films—silver halide, diazo, and vesicular.

Microfilm master copies usually are silver halide film, long

Figure 2

cartridges

Microfilm cartridges function as "convenience packaging" for rolls of microfilm. Unlike microfilm on reels, which require threading, cartridges can be self threading. Microfilm in cartridges is well protected, and not subject to fingerprints and other possible sources of damage.

ultrafiche

Ultrafiche contain images reduced more than 90X, thus permitting thousands of images per fiche. Ultrafiche offers the advantage of storing more information in less space than a standard microfiche.

aperture cards

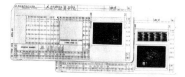

Available in many sizes—with the tab size (82.5mm x 187.25mm or 3¼" x 7⅜") most commonly used - - they combine key punched data and access information with microfilm. Aperture cards may contain a single image, or up to eight page-size images on one 35mm frame.

cassettes

Microfilm in cassettes gives added convenience to the handling of continuous rolls of microfilm. Each cassette contains two film cores—the feed and the take-up. There is no need to rewind a cassette when it is removed from the reader. Any frame may be held in viewing position for further reference at a later time.

jackets

A jacket is a plastic carrier with single or multiple sleeves or channels designed to accept strips of 16mm or 35mm film. Jackets both protect the microfilm and also facilitate organization of material. Images may be copied or read directly from the jacket without removing film. Jackets can be visibly titled for quick, easy file reference.

micro-opaques

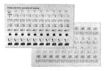

Similar to microfiche in configuration, micro-opaques are, as their name implies, images on opaque stock. Therefore, images may be stored on both sides. Unlike microfiche where transmitted light is used for blowback, opaques use reflected light.

Figure 3

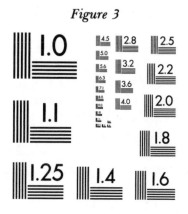

the primary composition in all types of photography because of its capability to record fine detail with minimum distortion. This capability to produce image quality—the quality of closely-spaced, fine lines on film—is evaluated in terms of resolving power. The National Bureau of Standards' Resolution Test Chart is used to measure the resolving power of microfilming systems. (Figure 3) This chart consists of 21 patterns ranging in spatial frequency from 1.0 to 10 lines per millimeter. The standard method of measuring the resolution of processed film is to examine the copy of the NBS Resolution Chart (which appears on processed microfilms) with the aid of a microscope set at a magnification of ⅓ to 1.0 times the resolving power (in cycles per millimeter) to be observed. For example, to examine 100 lines per millimeter, the magnification should be between 30 and 100 times. The numerical aperture of the microscope objective should not be less than 1/1000 of the resolving power to be measured. A pattern is considered to be resolved properly if the lines can be counted with certainty and if there are five lines in the pattern. If the camera were slightly out of focus, the number of lines per millimeter, on the smallest chart pattern in which the lines can be counted with certainty, multiplied by the reduction ratio gives the resolving power of the system. The ability to count the lines requires a clear distinction between the lines and the background. The fundamental concept of resolution is the ability of a system to produce separate images of closely-spaced objects. Thus, an essential requirement of a criterion of resolution is that the lines be separate.

The original silver halide photograph of any microfilmed document is called a first generation microfilm. After processing, the original is typically in negative polarity, i.e., print will appear as white images on a dark background. There are two common usages of the term polarity: (1) positive refers to a dark image on a white background, while *negative* refers to a white image on a dark background; and (2) *positive* refers to film which has the same tonal values as the original object (e.g., light areas on the original appear as light areas on the film; while negative refers to reversal of tonal values—light areas on originals appear dark on film, and dark areas on originals appear as light on film).

A large number of copies can be made from the first generation or original microfilm, and for many years the copies made on silver film from silver originals were sign reversing. The second generation film was positive—the reverse of the original negative. Kodak, however, developed a non-sign reversing silver halide film which produces negative copies from negative films and positive copies from positive films.

Silver halide film occupies a dominant position in original microfilm processing primarily because it is the only film for which archival tests and standards have been established.

Diazo

Diazo film takes its name from the process by which film is sensitized by diazonium salts. The film is processed with heat, ammonia and ultraviolet light in contact with a transparent original film, creating a duplicate of the original. Diazo is widely used to make intermediate or distribution copies for libraries and industry. It is much more resistant than silver film to damage from heat and scratching.

Vesicular

Vesicular is similar to diazo film in that diazonium compounds and ultraviolet light are utilized in its production. Unlike Diazo, the emulsion layer of vesicular film is plastic. When the diazonium salts are exposed to ultraviolet light they decompose, releasing nitrogen bubbles or vesicles. The plastic is softened by light or heat and vesicles are transformed into permanent images.

Vesicular film is highly durable, resists scratching and tearing, and fingerprints can be easily removed, as can other forms of dirt, oil, grease, etc. Since the film is processed with a plastic rather than gelatin layer, there is nothing to support bacterial or fungal growths and it is highly resistant to fading and discoloration in storage.

Cameras

The three basic cameras used in production of microforms are the flow type, planetary, and step and repeat cameras.

The *flow* or *rotary* type is commonly used with 16mm film. The document to be microfilmed is fed onto and compressed against a rotating drum. When the edge of the document revolves around the drum it trips a camera light and film advances. Images are exposed on the film as it passes behind a lens block. When the document exits, the movement of film ceases until another document is fed into the drum and the operation is repeated. Reduction ratios, or the ratio of the linear measurement of the document to the linear measurement of the microform image of that document, are controlled with interchangeable lens and corresponding film advancers. Reduction ratios are cited as 18×, 20×, 150×—meaning, in the latter example, that the document has been reduced to 1/150th of its original size.

With its automatic feed, the rotary camera is extremely fast, having the capability to record about 30,000 check size copies per hour.[1]

The *stand* or *planetary* camera is most often used with 35mm film, but can also accept film widths of 16mm, 70mm, and 105mm. The document to be filmed is placed on a stand and the camera is positioned on a raised column according to the size of the document and the desired reduction ratio. Reduction ratios decrease as the camera is lowered and they rise as the camera rises. Planetary cameras are equipped with light meters, positioning devices, and other components that ensure high quality, uniform exposures. While much slower than rotary cameras, planetary models are excellent for the production of

Figure 4

micrographics systems

As indicated on the preceding pages, there is a microfilm system that can be designed to meet your specific application. This chart brings these various component parts together to show the logical flow of a total microfilm system.

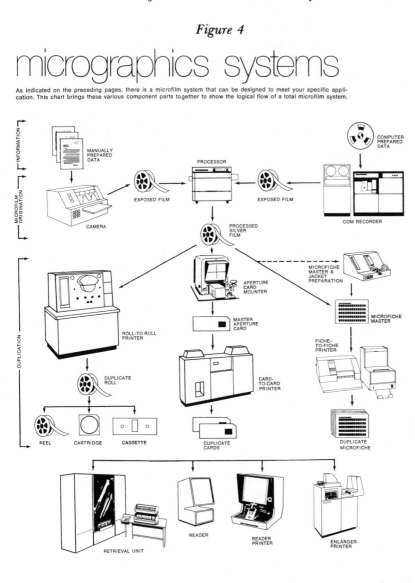

archival copies. It also is possible to process microfiche with a planetary camera by cutting the film and stripping it on microfiche jackets.

More often, however, *step and repeat* cameras are employed to make microfiche, with 70mm and 105mm film. The film is moved through the camera in sheet form, each movement being one frame length in duration automatically progressing from the top row to the second and so on until the sheet is completed. Author, title, and other information in the heading are photographed on the top edge of the fiche.

MICROFICHE

The attributes of microfiche were widely recognized in Europe decades prior to the selection of fiche for dissemination of technical report literature by the military and various civilian agencies of the U.S. Government, which gave impetus to the

Figure 5A

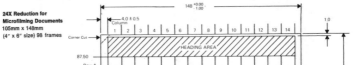

unitized microfilm formats

microfiche

The word "microfiche" is a combination of the prefix "micro" and the French word "fiche," meaning a file index card. The term microfiche refers to a sheet of microfilm containing multiple microimages in a grid pattern. It contains a heading (inscription placed at the top to identify its contents) which can be read without magnification.

A single microfiche may contain from a few images to several hundred, and as ultrafiche may retain many hundreds

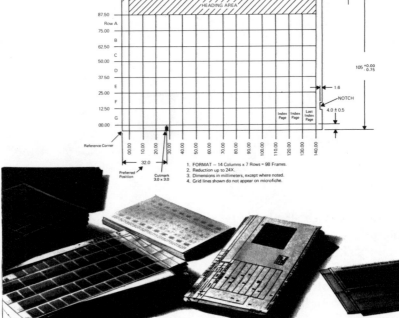

1. FORMAT — 14 Columns x 7 Rows = 98 Frames.
2. Reduction up to 24X.
3. Dimensions in millimeters, except where noted.
4. Grid lines shown do not appear on microfiche.

rapid acceptance of fiche in this country. Sheet microfilm was used in France and Germany prior to World War II, and the Microfiche Foundation in Holland, where microfiche originated, has carried on experiments with fiche for many years. "Card" was used to denote both sheet microfilm and micro-opaques until the British photographic expert, H.R. Verry, advocated the use of the word "card" only for micro-opaques.[2] His argument prevailed and thereafter "fiche" was used to categorize the 3 × 5 inch and 3½ × 4¾ inch sized sheets popular in Europe, and the 4 × 6 inch microfiche that has become fairly standard in the United States.

The 4 × 6 inch microfiche contains diverse numbers of frames or images depending on varying standards or manu-

Figure 5B

of images, depending on the reduction. The finished master fiche may be duplicated as a unit, rapidly and in any quantity.

The microfiche form of microfilm offers fast information retrieval. Microfiche may be designed to permit either manual retrieval (with an eye-legible identification at the top of a fiche) or automatic retrieval through edge notching or other machine-readable coding.

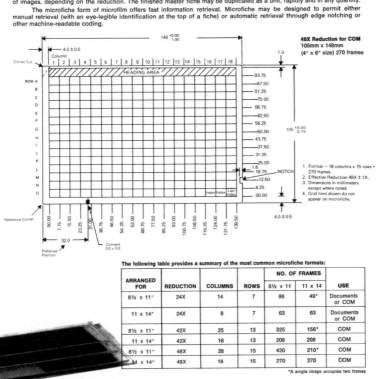

The following table provides a summary of the most common microfiche formats:

ARRANGED FOR	REDUCTION	COLUMNS	ROWS	NO. OF FRAMES 8½ x 11	NO. OF FRAMES 11 x 14	USE
8½ x 11"	24X	14	7	98	49*	Documents or COM
11 x 14"	24X	9	7	63	63	Documents or COM
8½ x 11"	42X	25	13	325	156*	COM
11 x 14"	42X	16	13	208	208	COM
8½ x 11"	48X	28	15	420	210*	COM
11 x 14"	48X	18	15	270	270	COM

*A single image occupies two frames

Figure 6

Image sizes and the number of images per fiche or per film reel
for 10 reduction ratios from 12X to 250X

At reduction ratio:	The image size would be (width x length):		The image to scale	No. of images (pages) per 4" x 6" fiche*	Rows by Columns		Approximate no. of images 100 ft. roll of film (comic mode)**
12X	18	x 23.3mm	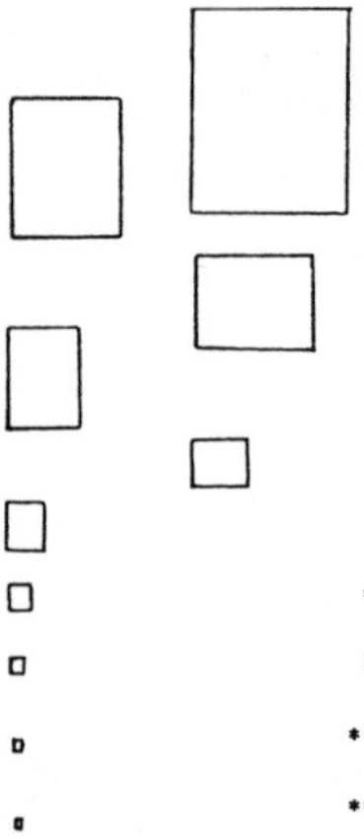	32	4	x 8	1,650
18X	12	x 15.5mm		72	6	x 12	2,500
20X	10.8	x 13.9mm		72	6	x 12	2,750
24X	9	x 11.6mm		112	8	x 14	3,300
42X	5.1	x 6.7mm		392	14	x 28	5,850
48X	4.5	x 5.8mm		**527	17	x 31	6,600
90X	2.4	x 3.1mm		**1,856	32	x 58	12,500
150X	1.44	x 1.6mm		**6,138	62	x 99	20,800
210X	1	x 1.33mm		**10,582	74	x 143	30,000
250X	.86	x 1.12mm		**14,685	89	x 166	34,600

* This page is 8½" x 11" (or, expressed metrically, 216mm x 279.4mm). Pages larger than 8½" x 11" would require larger images at the same reduction ratios. The number of images that can fit onto one microfiche depends on the reduction ratio used, the size of the microfiche or the length of the roll film, the size of the original page, and the amount of space given to margins, headers and spaces between images (i.e., non-image space).

** Ample space between images, especially in the higher reduction ratios and in roll microfilm, would tend to make these capacities impractical, but the table allows an idea of the comparable saturated capacities of the above reduction ratios for 4" x 6" fiche and 100 ft. long roll film.

facturer specifications. Examples are the Committee on Scientific and Technical Information (COSATI) microfiche of 60 frames (5 rows of 12 images), the National Micrographics Association (NMA) fiche of 98 frames (7 rows of 14 images), and the Bell and Howell fiche with 72 frames (6 rows of 12 images).

Reduction ratios employed with information sources on microform vary widely. Many government-sponsored technical reports (COSATI STANDARD) are filmed at one of the lowest common reduction ratios—18×. Books and serials published in fiche usually are reduced anywhere from 18–24 times. The publishing of the *Code of Federal Regulations* in fiche in 1975 was the spearhead of a mammoth offensive by the U.S. Government

Printing Office, whose original projections included offering 24× microfiche of all depository publications to depository libraries. Additionally, monographic collections offered by the National Cash Register Company and Library Resources, Incorporated, vary from 90× to 150×.

Although they usually are more expensive to produce than either microfilm or micro-opaques, microfiche are convenient to use and they provide better image resolution than opaques. Fiche are an attractive medium for original publishing in microform because of the low cost of duplication and mailing, and because fiche permit unitization of information. A single fiche often can hold an entire periodical issue, just as a single ultra-high reduction fiche is capable of presenting a large monograph. Fiche are inexpensive to replace if damaged or stolen, and they can be maintained in a number of storage configurations.

Aperture Cards

Microfiche also are used to present miniaturized information on aperture cards. A common application is to mount units of film over an aperture in a punched card for Hollerith, IBM, and other sorting machines.[3] The fast retrieval and unit record reproduction and filing made possible with aperture cards makes them particularly efficacious for storage of large documents, and the cards are widely used with engineering drawings and architectural maps.[4] The United States Government requires that drawings and other specifications be submitted on aperture cards with bids for defense contracts.

MICRO-OPAQUES

There are three basic types of micro-opaques: Microcards, Microprint, and Microlex.

Microcard is the form touted by Fremont Rider in the 1940s. The cards were typically 3 × 5 inches in size, and were printed by contact from 16mm or 35mm film which was cut and placed in correct position in about eighty frames on each side of a card. With the development of the step and repeat camera, the cost of producing microcards—already the least expensive microform to issue in large editions—was further reduced. Although they never attained the popularity predicted by Rider, microcards were used for many collections of research materials—among them the University of Oregon Health, Physical Education and Recreation (HPER) project of dissertation and other scholarly works in health, physical education, and recreation.

The Readex Microprint Corporation introduced the trade name Microprint to identify its 6 × 9 inch opaque card containing text (unlike microcard and microlex) printed by lithography on calendered paper. Microprint is neither a film transparency nor an opaque photographic print. The images (12–18×), of which about 100 appear on each microprint, are ink printed on card stock. Microprint meets the standard archival requirements of the National Bureau of Standards for paper and printing, having an optimum life span of more than 300 years. A wide variety of monographic, governmental, etc., collections have been offered on Microprint since 1950.

Microlex was first produced by the Lawyer's Co-operative Publishing Company for the specific purpose of making available to the legal profession out-of-print and prohibitively expensive monographs. Microlex are about 6½ × 8½ inches in size and contain two hundred images on each side of the card. Like microcards, microlex are produced photographically.

The chief disadvantage of opaques is their generally poor viewing quality. Unlike transparent film where transmitted light is used for blowback, opaques require reflected light for viewing. With film, a large percentage of light is transmitted from the film to the viewing screen. Opaque images must be illuminated so that light can be diffusely reflected from the paper to the screen. This handicap precludes the sharp images that are possible on fiche or film viewers and is responsible for frequent user complaints in libraries when long sessions with microcard viewers are necessary. Hard copy enlargements can be made from opaques,[5] but they also suffer in comparison with film enlargements. (Figure 7)

Despite the weak image quality of opaques, they are the least expensive microform, and they are remarkably resistant to damage from scratching or ill use. Both sides can be filled with print, and because of their durability the cards can be filed without envelopes.

Figure 7

HIGH AND ULTRA-HIGH
REDUCTION MICROFICHE

As we have seen, sheet sizes of conventional microfiche range from 3 × 5 inches to 5 × 8 inches, with the 4 × 6 inch achieving greatest popularity. Not all reading equipment will accept the multiplicity of card sizes, although the largest fiche size generally poses the only severe problem in providing compatible viewing machines. Variations in reduction ratio pose far greater complexity. Fiche conforming to COSATI standards range up to a maximum of 20×. The National Micrographics Association set standard ratios of fiche at 20× and 24×, while the American Library Association established standards of 14–20×. Viewers equipped with 18× lens are sufficient to read most documents filmed with reduction ratios between 14× and 24×, and many viewers can be supplied with variable lens although public service applications in libraries can suffer from the necessary delays and difficulties encountered in the changing of lens. A fiche viewer equipped with a 24× lens is excellent for reading material filmed at about 24×, but if a 14× document is blown back at 24×, the resulting image is so large as to require constant movement of the fiche carriage causing rapid fatigue and discomfort in continuous reading. Conversely, Computer Output Microfiche filmed at reduction ratios of 42×–48× can be read on a viewer equipped with a 24× lens but the characters are too small for anything but brief scanning or spot retrieval. The common solution in libraries is to provide viewers equipped with widely varying lens settings depending on the necessary applications. For, despite the increased costs, such flexibility is a necessary adjustment to an ungovernable plethora of microform offerings.

The development of ultrafiche transformed a relatively modest repast of fiche selections into a veritable banquet. Microform technology reached a stage where it seemed possible to reduce images to near infinity. If an ecclesiastical council could pronounce that the head of a pin would comfortably support x number of angels, then an ingenious microphotographer also could reproduce the Bible on a 1 × 1 inch sized microform.[6]

The first ultra-high reduction microfiche offered to libraries was the PCMI (photo-chromic-micro-image) Library Collections by the National Cash Register Company (NCR). The PCMI Collections consisted primarily of book length materials that were ill-adapted to filming in traditional microformats. For example, to be microphotographed at low reductions, a book of 1,000 pages would require one roll of film, ten Microprint sheets, or eleven NMA microfiche.[7] The advantages of unitizing books in microform for both reading and bibliographic control are readily apparent. It is far more convenient to retrieve, use, and refile one fiche for Gibbon's *Decline and Fall of the Roman Empire* than contend with ten or eleven separate units for the same work. But to make unitization a reality, it was necessary to use much higher reduction ratios. The PCMI collections were filmed at a reduction ratio of 150× on 4 × 6 Ultrafiche capable of holding over 3,000 pages of printed material. Ultrafiche are capable of holding not only one book but as many as ten or more separate bibliographical entities, and with PCMI the average number of entities per card averaged seven in number.[8]

NCR further expanded its ultrafiche offerings with the "College Bound Program." Whereas the PCMI Library Collections were intended for the college and university market, the "College Bound" series of "Essential Books" and "College Catalogs" were directed primarily to secondary school libraries and, to a lesser extent, to public libraries. NCR also produced a current bibliography of books in English combining the Library of Congress MARC data and entries from the British National Bibliography on Ultrafiche.

The NCR Ultrafiche publications were segregated into relatively small, clearly definable subject groupings, and libraries had the option of purchasing subject segments or the complete PCMI Library.

In the early 1970s a new library series was developed that was similar in scope to PCMI but differed in systems approach.

Library Resources, Incorporated (LRI), a subsidiary of Encyclopedia Britannica, produced its first in a projected series of large library collections—the Library of American Civilization (LAC). After substantial investment in research and development, LRI achieved unitization with high reduction microfiche. The 3 × 5 inch fiche in the Library of American Civilization each carry a maximum of 1,000 pages at reduction ratios varying from about 50× to 90×, such flexibility enabling the placement of no more than one bibliographic entity on any one fiche. The fiche were produced by photographing documents with a 35mm planetary camera at a low reduction ratio, and the 35mm film was then photographed again with a step and repeat camera employing a resolution capability of over 1,000 lines per millimeter.[9] The resulting master plates were used to print high quality dissemination copies.

The Library of American Civilization contains between 15,000 and 20,000 individual monographic titles and periodical articles about American history and life prior to 1914. Like the PCMI Library, LAC was designed for the academic market, particularly new or rapidly developing libraries that would have difficulty obtaining representative works in original editions or expensive reprints.

Unlike NCR, whose viewers could be equipped with dual lens to use low and ultra reduction microfiche, the Library of American Civilization required yet another line of viewers to read 50× to 90× reductions. Unfortunately, software and viewing equipment of the respective companies are mutually incompatible.

LAC and PCMI and their accompanying variety of desk top, portable, and reader/printer equipment are a step toward the "Duplicating Library" concept where vast and varied resources are always at the user's fingertips and nothing in a library is in circulation, missing, or at the bindery.[10] High and ultra-high reduction fiche collections provide significant savings in storage space in comparison with low reduction fiche; they are virtually immune to damage from scratching, fingerprints, and other abuse; and, if lost, they can be easily replaced. And surprisingly, for the user resistance devotee, high and ultra-high reduction microfiche often provide greater legibility and more convenient reading than the small, faded type of many original documents. That is not to say such collections are trouble free. Available readers (especially portable equipment) leave much to be desired. But with adequate indexing and catalog information, high reduction collections can be an asset to any library.

Although micropublishers make it possible for libraries to purchase almost any type of material, no matter how esoteric, in-house projects are not unknown. Some libraries own planetary cameras with which campus newspapers, financial records, theses, etc., are filmed and preserved. Others add special accessories to produce microfiche. A very few experiment with large scale, expensive progrms on the scale of Project Intrex at the Massachussets Institute of Technology, where library users are able to conduct literature searches on a CRT. Appropriate texts are called up from a microfiche file of resource texts, displayed on the CRT screen, and—if the user requests—hard copy reproductions are produced from the fiche texts.

Library underakings on the scale of Project Intrex are as rare as titled Microform Librarians. But as Computer Output Microfilm (COM) inches into the limelight it will open up a new era in file management, one that will see libraries revolutionized by shifts in processing activities, information retrieval, and public service.

The area of greatest change may not occur (as long expected) with microtexts and public services but instead with internal processing activities in libraries, where the tyranny of mass enjoyed by catalogues and other large files may be replaced by the domination of computers and microforms.

NOTES

1. Verry, H.R. *Microcopying Methods* (London: Focal Press, 1964), p. 175.

2. Viet, F. "Microforms, Microform Equipment, and Microform Use in the Educational Environment," *Library Trends* 19 (April 1971): 447–466.

3. Stevens, Guy. *Microphotography* (New York: Wiley, 1968), p. 510.

4. Avedon, Don. *Introduction to Micrographics* (Silver Spring, Md.: National Microfilm Association, 1973), p. 26.

5. Spaulding, Carl. "The Fifty Dollar Reading Machine and other Micromarvels," *Library Journal* (October 15, 1976), pp. 2134–2138.

6. Hawken, W.R. "Systems Instead of Standards," *Library Journal* 98 (September 15, 1973): 2515–25.

7. Evans, C.W. "High Reduction Microfiche for Libraries: An Evaluation of Collections from the NCR Company and LRI Inc," *Libraries Resources and Technical Services* 16 (Winter 1972): 33–47.

8. Doebler, P.D. "Libraries on microfiche: Library Resources inc's Experience in the Field," *Publishers Weekly* 202 (December 18, 1972): 27–30.

9. Williams, Bernard. *Miniaturized Communications* (London: The Library Association, 1970), p. 190.

10. Grieder, E.M. "Ultrafiche Libraries: A Librarian's View," *Microform Review* 1 (April 1972): 85–100.

Chapter 3

Computer Output Microfilm

Computer Output Microfilm (COM) is the process of recording output from a computer directly onto film with microimages instead of the traditional paper copy commonly produced on impact printers. Impact printers appear to operate at a terrific rate of speed. Actually they are much, much slower than the computers generating the data. After the printing is completed, the paper printout must be decollated, burst, and bound, which takes as much time as the actual printing. If more than six copies are required, the entire operation must be repeated. The printouts are heavy, awkward to use, and expensive to mail or distribute. COM, on the other hand, is about twenty times faster than an impact printer. While the computer is generating data at a rate of 500,000 characters per second, ordinary line printers work at a capability of about 6,000 characters per second. By substituting a COM recorder for the line printer, data transmission can be increased from 6,000 to more than 120,000 characters per second. Thus expensive computer time is utilized much more efficiently with COM than with impact printers.[1]

Data generated by a COM recorder can be stored at packing densities twenty-five to one hundred times greater than magnetic tape and disk storage and at a compression ratio of five hundred to one compared to paper storage. Low costs of generating data, ease of handling and storage, and substantially reduced expenses of mailing and distribution grant COM significant advantages over tape or disk storage and paper reports.

The evolution of COM technology began in the late 1940s when Stromberg-Carlson Corporation produced the Charactron shaped beam tube, a highly sophisticated cathode ray

Figure 8

THE CHARACTRON® SHAPED BEAM TUBE

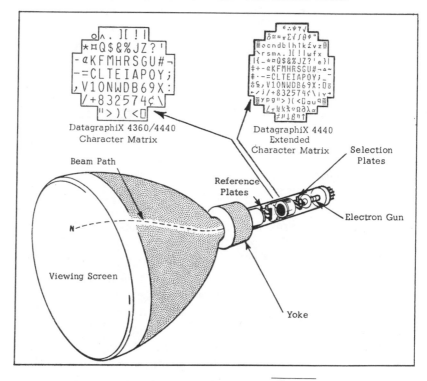

®Registered, Stromberg DatagraphiX

tube (CRT) capable of displaying graphic and alphanumeric data with extraordinary precision and clarity at speeds of hundreds of thousands of characters per second.[2] (Figure 8) To explain the operation of a CRT with a gross oversimplification, it can be stated that an electron beam is projected through a matrix of special characters etched onto a metal disk. As the electron beam makes contact with the phosphor-coated face of a CRT, the designated character or characters light up on the screen. This equipment was first used in radars of the U.S. Air Force's Early Warning System.

During the mid-1950s, the Stromberg-Carlson devices were combined with a microfilm camera to create the first COM recorders, equipment that converted data from a computer into human readable language subsequently recorded onto microfilm. The first commercial COM unit was installed at Convair Aerospace in San Diego in 1961 and was used to process data for the early Atlas missiles.

COM development proceeded slowly during the following years with IBM operating a COM unit for the Social Security Administration and with other companies such as 3M, Memorex, and Kodak, joining the field. The 3M unit consisted of a six milliwatt helium neon laser beam producing characters directly onto 3M Dry Silver 16mm microfilm or 105mm microfiche, and forming latent images in reduction ratios of 25×, 42×, or 48× by heat rather than by chemicals. The 3M system produced, in microform, the equivalent of two to five pages of paper printout per second. Memorex, on the other hand, formed alphanumeric characters by lighting up 5 × 7 matrix arrays of photodioxide strands. Characters were activated by direct digital control, rapidly photographed, and then advanced to accept a new line of characters. The distinguishing feature of this system was the use of optical fibers to carry light within the photodiode strands.[3]

Although there are differing characteristics, the various COM recorders on the market today do have a number of basic functional traits in common. These are:

1. An *input* section to receive binary data from the computer, either from a magnetic tape transport (off-line) or directly from the computer mainframe (on-line).
2. A *logic* section where the input data is interpreted and subjected to logic conversion for generation of signals to produce film manipulation, output, formatting, titling, and index extraction.
3. A *conversion* section where binary data is converted to the analog signals required to drive deflection and display sections that convert the data to human readable alphanumeric or graphic displays.
4. A *deflection* section that controls the positioning of images on a CRT or directly onto film.
5. A *display* section to convert computer-generated data into human readable form with a CRT, Electron-Beam Recording, Light-Emitting Diodes, or Laser Beam Recording.

Figure 9A

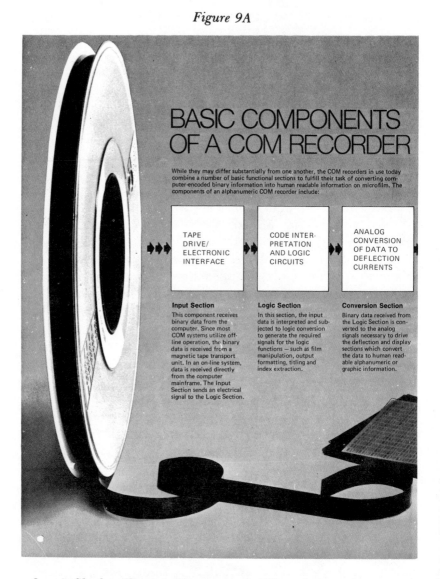

BASIC COMPONENTS OF A COM RECORDER

While they may differ substantially from one another, the COM recorders in use today combine a number of basic functional sections to fulfill their task of converting computer-encoded binary information into human readable information on microfilm. The components of an alphanumeric COM recorder include:

TAPE DRIVE/ ELECTRONIC INTERFACE	CODE INTER-PRETATION AND LOGIC CIRCUITS	ANALOG CONVERSION OF DATA TO DEFLECTION CURRENTS

Input Section

This component receives binary data from the computer. Since most COM systems utilize off-line operation, the binary data is received from a magnetic tape transport unit. In an on-line system, data is received directly from the computer mainframe. The Input Section sends an electrical signal to the Logic Section.

Logic Section

In this section, the input data is interpreted and sub-jected to logic conversion to generate the required signals for the logic functions — such as film manipulation, output formatting, titling and index extraction.

Conversion Section

Binary data received from the Logic Section is con-verted to the analog signals necessary to drive the deflection and display sections which convert the data to human read-able alphanumeric or graphic information.

6. A *film handling* section encompassing a lens and exposure and film handling mechanisms. Here images are photographically reduced in size and recorded on film.[4]

The film output may be any one of the standard formats—fiche, or roll microfilm on reels, cartridges, or cassettes—though not all brands of COM recorders are capable of pro-

Figure 9B

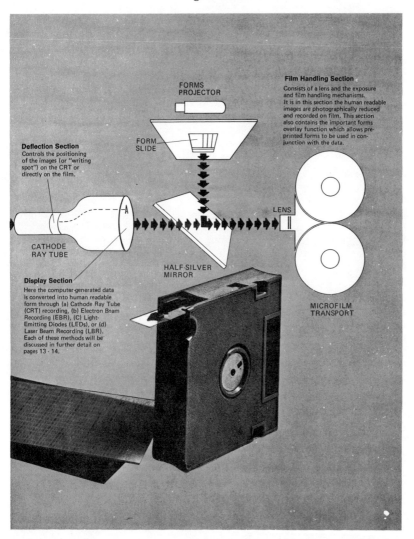

Film Handling Section
Consists of a lens and the exposure
and film handling mechanisms.
It is in this section the human readable
images are photographically reduced
and recorded on film. This section
also contains the important forms
overlay function which allows pre-
printed forms to be used in conjunction with the data.

FORMS
PROJECTOR

FORM
SLIDE

Deflection Section
Controls the positioning
of the images (or "writing
spot") on the CRT or
directly on the film.

LENS

CATHODE
RAY TUBE

HALF-SILVER
MIRROR

Display Section
Here the computer-generated data
is converted into human readable
form through (a) Cathode Ray Tube
(CRT) recording, (b) Electron Beam
Recording (EBR), (C) Light-
Emitting Diodes (LEDs), or (d)
Laser Beam Recording (LBR).
Each of these methods will be
discussed in further detail on
pages 13 - 14.

MICROFILM
TRANSPORT

ducing all formats. A special camera attachment is required to
produce microfiche from 105mm film, while engineering drawings on 35mm film have been generated on aperture cards.
Many different reduction ratios are available. The most typical
are 24× (98 page images on 4 × 6 inch fiche) and 42× (about
208 printout size page images or about 225 8½ × 11 inch pages
on 4 × 6 inch fiche).

Other units assembled in COM systems may include film developers, film duplicators to produce multiple copies of the film or fiche end product, storage units to house film, and readers and reader-printers to make hardcopy from the microform.

Sixteen millimeter or 35mm microfilm was used in early COM applications, but as microfiche gained wider acceptance, 105mm cameras were designed to run roll film for microfiche formats. These cameras (called "universal") were adapted to use 16 and 35mm as well.

Machine or punched card set-up controls can govern the re-

Figure 10A

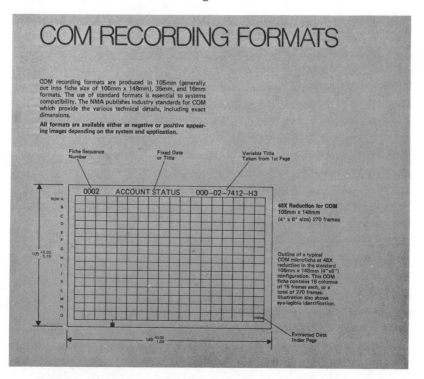

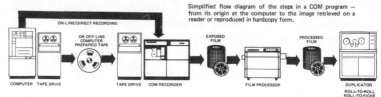

duction ratio, column and row advance, and page sequence in fiche production. Page sequences on the fiche ordinarily flow from the top to bottom of each column, with the columns running from left to right. Different formatting is possible, but COM business applications ordinarily use a sequential listing to allow rapid access to the desired information.

The film used in COM recorders differs from regular silver halide microfilm in that a special emulsion is added to match the color of CRT phosphor screens. Characters show up on the screen as white lines on a dark background (positive). If nega-

Figure 10B

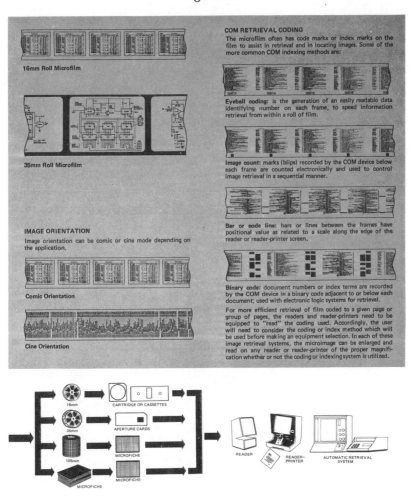

tive polarity is desired, distribution prints can be processed with a reversing copy, silver or vesicular film. Diazo duplicates are non-reversing so they will turn out positive if the original is positive.

Vesicular duplicating film has gained favor in COM applications because it produces a negative image from a positive master. And, since it is heat developed, no darkroom or wet processing is necessary.

COM is a rapidly developing market. With new service bureaus and equipment manufacturers entering the field, project-

Figure 10C

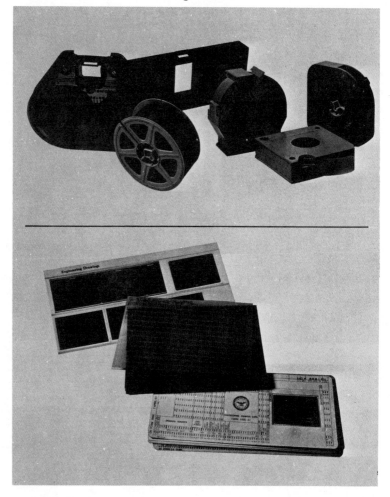

ing the state of the art for COM is like pinpointing the exact volume of ocean displaced by a space vehicle on reentry. Formats, image orientations, film sizes, film transports, etc., vary widely depending on the type of equipment and the specific application.

Some of the earliest commercial COM applications surfaced in spare parts and catalog stores (e.g., Sears Roebuck placed all its spare parts lists on microfiche), hospital and insurance records, telephone listings, and state automobile registration lists. (The state of Illinois reduced its list from seventeen printed

Figure 10D

OPERATIONAL CONSIDERATIONS FOR THE COM PROGRAM

The prospective COM user may find a large number of different modes of operation of the COM systems under consideration. Our purpose here is to provide you with a brief explanation of some of these operational considerations to assist you in your COM system evaluation. As mentioned previously, the growing COM market is well served by a number of manufacturers, and mention of a particular mode of operation here does not constitute an endorsement. Also, the lack of mention of a mode of operation can doubtlessly be ascribed to emerging technologies that render any such reference work somewhat out of date as it rolls off the presses.

Mode of Operation—On-Line or Off-Line

Two types of systems are used to provide the digital data — On-Line and Off-Line, with the latter the most commonly used in present Computer Output Microfilm applications.

The Off-Line COM method can be considered the same as an off-line printer operation. The computer generates the data which is coded onto magnetic tape, which is in turn brought off-line to the COM device which produces the microfilm. Off-line offers three specific advantages which make it more desirable from an operational standpoint: separate operation, programming flexibility, and greater capability.

- **Separate Operation** — frees the computer from the output recorder, allowing the tape to be rerun as many times as necessary without having to go back to the main frame computer.

- **Programming Flexibility** — means, simply, that a single Off-Line COM machine can handle many different input formats and can process information generated by many different types of computers.

- **Greater Capability** — especially important in graphics work. The Off-Line COM unit acts as a plotter to generate the graphics, freeing the main computer for other data functions. For example, in generating a graphic curve, the main computer provides the end points and allows the COM unit to draw the vector. Because many Off-Line COM recorders incorporate internal mini-computers and software, graphics can be produced most economically in this mode of operation.

In On-Line systems, the data goes directly from the main frame computer to the COM recorder, eliminating the need for magnetic tape units. This can reduce equipment cost. With On-Line systems most of the software and memory is provided by the main frame. This mode of operation also facilitates quicker reference to the final material, since it is not necessary to record on an intermediate magnetic tape.

As can be seen, each method offers its advantages, and the ultimate decision must be based on a combination of specific application and expenditure.

On-Line COM

Off-Line COM

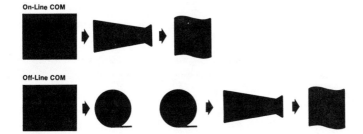

books to one hundred fiche at a fifty percent savings.) As was true of the development of microforms in general, the acceptance and growth of COM was assured in commerce and industry long before libraries experimented with suitable applications. The earliest wide scale implementation occurred in Europe. As early as 1967, the Westminster, England city libraries, in a joint project with other nearby cities, began a computer catalog project that by 1971 produced COM catalogs for interlibrary-loan and public service functions.[5] Memorex microfilm viewers were used to read the microfilm catalogs. Buckle and Thomas reported in 1972 that four English county library systems were utilizing COM catalogs, four more were planning systems, one city library and one national library had operational COM systems, and one polytechnic library had microfilmed its card catalog and made it available in cassettes. Additional projects to be completed before the end of 1972 were the microfilming of catalog cards by a national library, an unidentified COM experiment by one university library, and the choice of 16mm microfilm cassettes by Birmingham University for its COM-produced catalog.[6]

One very early COM operation in the United States was implemented in 1966 by Lockheed Missiles and Space Library in Palo Alto, California.[7] Catalog information for new books and reports was keypunched and transferred to magnetic tape. The catalogs were then COM-produced on 16mm microfilm in cartridges containing about 25,000 entries each and distributed to scientists and engineers at Lockheed plants in Palo Alto and elsewhere.

During 1970/71 public libraries began jumping into COM with as much enthusiasm as Melville Dewey promoting spelling reforms one hundred years before. A report on the Los Angeles Public Library's COM operation described production of COM reports for a "patron directory" of all registered library users, a "delinquent report" of patrons who did not return library materials or pay fines and fees, a "system open order report" of all materials currently on order, and a "book history report," a cumulative record of all the titles ordered since the implementation of the library's automated order system in 1967.[8] The bulk of paper generated in these reports prior to COM created massive storage and handling problems, even to the extent of precluding distribution to interested users. Extensive time was needed to print and distribute the reports, and the consequent delays in distribution detracted from the timeliness and value of the reported data. There were instances of patrons receiving overdue notices and calling on the library to contest fines before the library staff had received the current "delinquent report." And, of course, costs of producing paper printouts were astronomical. The price of one "book history report" was close to $5,000.

When Los Angeles Public converted to COM catalogs (fiche instead of film primarily because of lower costs with fiche), the much smaller size of catalogs made comprehensive distribution possible, at least two clerical positions were saved, delivery time speeded so that the "delinquent report" was available twenty-four hours after updating compared to the previous paper delay of two weeks, and $100,000 was saved during each year of operation. User reaction was reported as "preponderately favorable" and the Library planned to expand COM application to book shelf lists, serial holdings, and other public service tools.

The Hennepin County Public Library (Minneapolis, Minnesota) adopted COM for its on-order files and book history reports. A 1,350 page paper report costing $1,000 became with COM a few fiche at $100. And the Louisiana Library Association created a COM union catalog in 42× fiche containing locations at that time for more than one million volumes in twenty-one Louisiana libraries, certainly a boon to interlibrary loan.[9] Georgia Tech produced COM fiche catalogs (42×) for book and serial holdings. Yale used a COM biweekly in-process list on cartridge-loaded 28× microfilm. The University of North Carolina at Raleigh and Mankato State University (Minnesota) separately created COM serials catalogs of five microfiche (42×). The University of Michigan (at Saline) and the University of Colorado used COM for circulation and in-process files. Washington University School of Medicine tried COM for book catalogs. Wayne State University distributed a COM union list of serials in 16mm microfilm cassettes. Some other early converts to COM user ranks included Newark Public, University of Wisconsin–Milwaukee, University of Pittsburgh, Wright State, Boeing Corporation, El Centeo Junior College, NASA, Tulane, Santa Clara County Free Library, National Scurity Agency, and Timberland Regional Library in Olympia, Washington.

Other large scale commercial COM projects were started by

Information Design which marketed a catalog supply service utilizing microfilm versions of each card in MARC records. This service, called *CARDSET,* was a COM-produced set of title/ series and Library of Congress (LC) number indexes to the MARC files provided on 16mm microfilm cartridges from which libraries could produce complete sets of LC catalog cards on XEROX microprinters. The British National Bibliograpy (BNB) advertised *Books in English,* a set of 150× ultra-microfiche containing catalog information on all English language books cataloged by BNB or the Library of Congress. Crowell, Collier, McMillan offered *PANDEX,* a biweekly index to science, engineering, and medical literature, on COM-generated microfiche, while the Library of Congress produced its *SUBJECT HEADNGS* on 24× microfiche.

Other micropublishing projects followed as primary interest for COM library applications centered on production of catalogs. Alternatives to the traditional card catalog became feasible as automated services became increasingly available to libraries. The larger the catalog, the more expensive maintenance became as entries were established and differentiated from other headings in the catalog. Consistency and accuracy in old, large catalogs left much to be desired, as did the physical condition of card stock after prolonged use. Physical space to house a catalog, filing of cards and file revision, staff costs for maintenance—all were serious problems, but perhaps the most serious disadvantage of all was the relative inaccessibility of a union card catalog which was usually available only in one location in a campus or regional library setting.[10]

A number of libraries, particularly small and medium-sized public libraries, replaced card catalogs with computer-generated book catalogs. Branch libraries could then use the same union catalog that was formerly available only at the regional center. Though very expensive, these book catalogs were less costly than maintaining individual catalogs for all branch libraries.[11]

When COM technology became available to libraries, the high cost of producing book catalogs was reduced by converting from paper to microform. Auto-Graphics, Inc., Science Press, Information Design, Inc., etc., developed COM-generated microfilm catalogs. These companies converted author, title and subject entries for books in library card catalogs into machine readable form by utilizing MARC records. A new catalog was thus produced on microfilm accessed through a table top LCR 500 microfilm reader developed by Auto-Graphics (loaded with 16mm roll film up to five hundred feet in length) or the similar ROM 2 microfilm viewer marketed by Information Design. Both readers were equipped with automatic controls and index-ing devices that made rapid bibliographic searching possible.

At the nation's largest library and primary source of catalog data, growth of the MARC data base and progress on systma-tizing processing activities moved the Library of Congress steadily closer to fully automated bibliographic files.[12] By 1979 the Library hoped to increase the MARC data base to more than a million and a half records to be accessed on-line (e.g., with the aid of CRT's or through COM-generated microform catalogs). For fastest response, users could access on-line biblio-graphic records from name, subject, title, and call number files. For less urgent access, batch processing and microform output would be sufficient. Projections placed the 1979 size of the li-brary's main card catalog at 22 million cards, with an annual rate of growth near one million cards. Maintaining such a gigantic catalog could require a staff of seventy, with salaries totaling more than $600,000 annually. Continuing to enter new cards in the catalog would create indefensible duplication since all current cataloging would be converted to, and available in, MARC. What would become of the venerable card catalog? Suspended animation. It would be closed and used only as a reference source. Name headings, subject headings, and call numbers would be established solely from MARC records. Manual access would be replaced by fully automated systems, allowing the user to search files with much greater flexibility and speed than was ever possible with the card catalog.

Other libraries quickly followed suit. Those who closed or planned to close card catalogs included New York Public, Ohio State, University of Texas, National Library of Canada, State University of New York, Brigham Young, New York State, and Northwestern. Many of these libraries planned to keep their card catalogs for retrospective searches and to use a COM cata-log for all additions after closing off old catalogs. Users would be confronted by two access points—one for resources acquired before a given date and another for materials received after that date. Others, like Georgia Tech, filmed all entires in the "old" catalog and produced COM supplements for new additions.[13] Each bimonthly supplement cited additions and revisions made to the card catalog since it was filmed, with each supplement superseding all previous supplements. Both the basic file and the supplements were microfiche, divided into author-title, subject, and serials sections, and distinguished by color coding and numbering for ease in filing them (717 fiche) in the basic file.

Despite the problems of maintaining large fiche files compared to the apparently greater ease of controlling file integrity with microfilm cassettes and cartridges on motorized readers, the economic features of microfiche were indisputable signposts for many libraries confused by unfamiliar terrain. The salient characteristic of COM catalogues is portability. Copies can be distributed to all branch libraries, to every department in a library, nay, even to every department in a campus—as long as readers are available to view the microform catalogs. Good fiche readers can be purchased for one-fifth the price of a comparable film reader, a fact very few libraries are able to ignore with impunity. At Georgia Tech's library, which purchased readers to accompany COM catalogs on locations around the campus, microfiche was considered superior to film in terms of simplicity and realiability. The fiche readers were among the simplest available to use and maintain, and file organization made it possible to find and display any entry in the catalog within seconds. "Extensive comparison and testing of the self-indexing microfiche approach with mechanized systems and external indexes" convinced Georgia Tech staff that "the microfiche system has greater reliability, is simpler to understand and use, and provides as fast or faster access, as well as requiring less expensive readers." The expense of producing COM catalogs was cited as less than one-tenth the cost of the same number of copies in book form.

Still other libraries, utilizing the vast resources of the Ohio College Library Center (OCLC), created COM catalogues based on the voluminous data base of records available from that system. The University of Texas at Dallas converted its catalog from card stock to COM-generated microfiche, using catalog data from OCLC and Blackwells/North America.[14]

Bierman's study of automated alternatives to card catalogues revealed that libraries do acknowledge the eventual replacement of card catalogs by computer systems, especially as the costs of card catalogs continue to climb and costs of computers continue to fall. Large research libraries anticipated adoption of on-line systems as technology and economics permit, perhaps within ten years. Large public libraries believed that printed book or microform catalogs would be used for some time to come, even though on-line catalogs were the optimum choice. A majority of the libraries argued for a printed book or microform catalog to serve as a physical backup to on-line catalogs. On that basis the question is not whether libraries will convert to microform catalogs, but whether the format of such catalogs will be film or fiche. Despite widespread advocacy of microfilm cassettes and cartridges as the most convenient and fastest form to access, Bierman's survey reflected use of fiche COM catalogs in nine out of ten libraries. Five of the ten libraries in the survey were academic, three special, and only two public. Since Bierman's survey, additional public libraries have converted to COM catalogs, usually microfilm. Because file integrity is simplest to ensure with microfilm cartridges and cassettes, public libraries may grant more weight to this factor than other types of libraries. However, libraries using fiche reported high user acceptance and little difficulty in maintaining file integrity.

Whatever the outcome of the debate over fiche and film, one thing is certain. Computer output microfilm has the capability to save libraries large sums of money while enhancing the services provided to users. On that basis, continued and widespread development of COM in libraries is assured.

NOTES

1. *Computer Output Microfilm Industry* (Mountain View, Ca.: Quantor Corporation, nd), p. 27.

2. *Computer Output Microfilm* (Washington, D.C.: General Services Administration, 1975), p. 46.

3. "Computer Output Microfilm," *Advanced Technology/Libraries* (May 1972), pp. 1–8.

4. *Fundamentals of Computer Output Microfilm* (Silver Springs, Md.: National Microfilm Association, 1974), p. 23.

5. Lakeworthy, Graham and Brown, Cyril. "Library Catalogs on Microfilm," *Library Association Record* (December 1971): 231–32.

6. Buckle, D.R.G. and French, Thomas. "The Application of Microform to Manual and Machine Readable Catalogues," *Program* 6 (July 1972): 187–203.

7. Kozumplik, William A. and Lange, R.T. "Computer Produced Microfilm Library Catalog," *American Documentation* 18: (April 1967): 67–80.

8. Fischer, Mary L. "The Use of Com at Los Angeles Public Library," *The Journal of Micrographics.* 6 (May 1973): 205–210.

9. Bolef, Doris. "COM," *Special Libraries* 65 (April 1974): 169–175.

10. Elrod, J. McRee. "Is the Card Catalogue's Unquestioned Sway in North America Ending?" *The Journal of Academic Librarianship* 2 (March 1976): 4–8.

11. Bierman, Kenneth John. "Automated Alternatives to Card Catalogs: The Current State of Planning and Implementation," *Journal of Library Automation* 8 (December 1975): 277–298.

12. Rather, John C. "The Future of Catalog Control in the Library of Congress," *Journal of Academic Librarianship* 1 (May 1975): 4–7.

13. Roberts, Edward G. and Kennedy, John P. "The Georgia Tech Library's Microfiche Catalog," *Journal of Micrographics* (July 1973) pp. 245–251.

14. Meyer, Richard W. and Knapp, J.F. "COM Catalog Based on OCLC Records," *Journal of Library Automation* 8 (December 1975): 312–321.

Chapter 4

Serials in Microform

Newspapers, periodicals, and other publications issued serially, i.e., printed and distributed at regular intervals, are available in a wide range of formats from a large and rapidly increasing number of micropublishers.[1]

Newspapers may be the only item where, by general acclaim, microreproductions are favored and given almost complete priority in libraries. The added convenience to the reader of having newspapers on microform is attributed to the increased size of the type appearing on the screen, sharper and more clearly defined characters, faster service, working quarters uncluttered by the chaff that constantly falls from decaying wood pulp paper, and the elimination of volumes that weigh anywhere from seventeen to twenty-five pounds.[2]

Although space saving has been regarded as less important than added convenience of use in converting newspapers to microform, it is possible to store an entire run of the *New York Times* on microfilm in fewer than one-half dozen medium-sized file cabinets. When an adequate index is available, as with the *Times*, access to a microfilm run is rapid indeed. Because of the length of files involved and the spot searching typical of newspaper research, 16 and 35mm microfilm is conveniently handled on motorized viewers. Thousands of newspapers have been offered for sale by Bell and Howell, some of special interest such as Contemporary Newspapers of the North American Indian, others of general interest with comprehensive indexing such as the *Chicago Tribune, Los Angeles Times, New Orleans Times–Picayune,* and *Washington Post.* Microfilming Corporation of America and other micropublishers offer many additional newspapers on 16 or 35mm microfilm reels—the format that most readers and librarians seem to prefer. And accompanying book indexes offer rapid and uncomplicated access to the world's most important newspaper literature.

As for periodicals, several factors are responsible for the increased conversion of magazines to microform. The rapid rise in costs, with subscription prices climbing sixty percent between 1957 and 1968,[3] and one hundred and sixty percent from 1969 to 1976,[4] forced libraries to drastically reduce the size of subscription lists. The worst years of price increases coincided with the great enrollment decline in higher education during the early seventies, when funding for library materials was slashed in private arts colleges, state universities, and even the wealthiest and most prestigious institutions in the country. At the same time that vast hordes of graduate students were seeking more extensive research materials, libraries were compelled to make do with less of everything. It was not unusual to see periodical holdings in many libraries reduced dramatically, seemingly overnight.

Forced to seek alternatives, libraries increasingly turned to networking and inter-library loan for the materials they could no longer afford to buy and make available in-house. One group of small liberal arts colleges in the Midwest of the United States pooled the resources of member libraries and created a central bank of core periodical titles (mainly microfilm) whose articles could be photocopied and returned to patrons within three days after a request was transmitted to the bank. The venture was funded by grants and by proceeds from the sale of periodical runs owned in duplicate by participating libraries.[5] This system provided an exceptional variety of periodical literature to its member libraries, but its influence was diminished by steadily increasing operating costs and the formation of state-wide networks.

One of the earliest and most successful networks was the Minnesota Interlibrary Telecommunications Exchange (MINITEX). Funded by legislative action, MINITEX was housed in the state's largest research library, at the University of Minnesota, and had as its goal the rapid dissemination of monographic and periodical literature to college students throughout Minnesota. Requests for articles that were unavailable in academic libraries were teletyped to Minneapolis, and photocopies were returned by courier or Greyhound bus. A special aspect of this project was the creation of a Minnesota Union List of Serials which pinpointed resources of the state's libraries.

The success of MINITEX was followed by similar ventures in Wisconsin and other states. Access to vast quantities of periodical literature at minimal cost through these networks was an attractive lifeline for hard-pressed acquisition librarians. Titles could be cut from subscription lists and new offerings passed up as long as access was assured through some form of interlibrary loan, but gradually publishers began to complain of copyright infringement and warned that the increased reliance on cooperative acquisitions among groups of libraries was forcing prices upward to compensate for declining sales. Some publishers resorted to charging consortia significantly higher subscription rates to make up for the loss in sales that they claimed resulted from pooling of library resources.

Nevertheless, librarians continued to expand networking. One writer argued that it was less expensive for libraries to borrow rather than buy journals with an average subscription price of twenty dollars if the frequency of use was less than 5.4 times per year.[6] His proposed solution to providing readers with ready access to all of the publications they needed was to create a national lending collection that could provide publications used "so infrequently that many libraries can share the use of the same copy without undue conflict." In 1975 the Center for Research Libraries began just such a program, called the "Journals Access Service." It began providing photocopies of any article in the fields of science, social science, or the humanities, with a publication date of 1970 or later. The Center supplied photocopies to member libraries within three to ten days, depending on whether or not the article was available from the Center or from the affiliated services of the huge interlibrary loan system at the British Library Lending Division.

The growth of interlibrary loan, which started as a means of providing esoteric and unique research sources, toward state wide systems and national networks enabled students to gain access to information that at one time even professors may have found unobtainable. One of the most significant achievements came in the area of undergraduate studies where students could be introduced very early to scholarly investigation and sophisticated scientific research with the certainty that adequate documentation was available to support their work despite the often pathetic condition of the local library. This writer recalls one senior at a liberal arts college who completed an advanced honors project in pre-medicine *summa cum laude,* in spite of his library's possession of fewer than one dozen relevant medical journals. His work was based almost entirely on photocopies of articles from American, English, Australian, and even Indian medical journals.

Although networking alleviated the difficulty of gaining adequate access to periodical literature, other problems continued to plague serial librarians. If librarians occasionally heard user complaints about long delivery lags and the failure to build impressive at-hand research collections, a much more serious and omnipresent lament concerned theft and multilation. Never bore periodical librarians with descriptions of how versatile the uses of a lowly razorblade are. Book losses through theft are a major concern, but add to that the ravages of mutilation to which periodicals are so mercilessly prone and you have a seemingly hopeless situation. Maintaining closed stacks precludes losses from theft and mutilation. But staffing such systems can cost more than twice as much as the total cost of obtaining replacements.[7] And the thought of restricting access to materials (including the denial of browsing) is repugnant to many service oriented librarians who are trying to forget the heritage of libraries formidable as monasteries and just as austere. Tipping in replacement issues seems a small enough price to pay for the luxury of maintaining open collections.

Yet, there are times when even the most generous librarian is tempted to padlock periodicals. Hendrick and Murfin[8] found that periodical mutilation feeds on itself. As missing issues are discovered by users they tend to vent frustration and anger by tearing further articles out of an issue which they consider to be already ruined. Users also believed periodicals to be "cheap" in comparison with books. Replacements, especially, were believed to be inexpensive. Offenders admitted that "laziness" was responsible for much mutilation, but other factors contributed as well. Copy machines that were incapable of reproducing maps or fine print or color, no available change, lack of opportunities for overnight checkout, early closing times, and pure and simple "orneriness" were also cited. The study indicated that overnight checkouts, good inexpensive copiers, and forceful publicity about the costs of obtaining replacements will do much to reduce theft and mutilation.

In addition to all the other problems they cause, ruined and missing issues make it that much more difficult to preserve materials by maintaining one of a library's most expensive programs: binding. After acquisitions, binding constitutes the most expensive operation in a periodicals department. There is the constant review of titles to be made ready for binding, the elaborate recod keeping on color format, frequency, indexes, etc., the packing and shipping and reshelving of volumes—all requiring an incredible attention to detail that only experienced staff seem able to provide. Hence, there are not only commercial binding charges to contend with (and inflation has pushed paper and buckram rapidly higher) so that libraries routinely can spend one-third as much for commercial binding as they do for annual subscription fees, but also there are the many salary dollars to be allocated for librarians and clerks who move volumes through the binding process. A number of small, inexpensive binding machines have been marketed with indifferent results, their chief advantage being the reduced cost of bringing together loose issues.

Another enormous expense is generated by collection growth and the need for more and larger library buildings. Over a billion dollars went into construction of new academic libraries between 1967 and 1974. This created space for 163 million volumes, but during the same period libraries added more than 167 million volumes.[9] The Great Enrollment Decline brought a New Library Construction Decline but new books and periodicals continued to spill onto the shelves at a rate that lends credibility to Rider's theory of libraries doubling in size every sixteen years.[10] At 1975 collection maintenance costs of twenty cents per volume, research libraries were spending hundreds of thousands of dollars each year on maintenance alone. Energetic weeding and remote storage were poor but necessary substitutes for new facilities.

The high costs of subscriptions and binding—plus the added

trauma of theft and shrinking shelf space—are not new problems for periodical librarians, but these factors have been rudely exacerbated by inflation and reduced funding. Microform editions of serials, available in good numbers at least as early as 1941 from University Microfilms and other micropublishers, were utilized sparingly in libraries chiefly as a means of reducing storage requirements. Only recently, as dollars dwindled, have microforms gained increasing favor for other features of economy. Periodicals on microform, saving over ninety percent of space required to shelve paper issues, eliminate the need to bind loose issues.[11] A typical bibliographical title is converted into approximately two physical bound volumes each year. Since the average price of a microform edition is only slightly more than the average cost of binding one class A volume, these substantial savings combined with diminished demand for storage space, provide compelling economic logic for the conversion of back files to microform. Add to that the reduced danger of theft and mutilation (despite reports from some libraries of certain frames missing from the microform runs of Playboy, etc.) and the consequently smaller student labor force required to reshelve volumes after use. (This is another of the staff costs generally overlooked when considering expenditure for periodicals. Keeping volumes on the shelf and in the correct order is a constant trial for all involved.)

Total operating costs of maintaining periodicals on microform begin to approach, if not a manageable level, at least one that can be far below the costs of a traditional bound collection. This recognition spurred additional publishers into action. Princeton, Plenum, AMS, Springer-Verlag, John Wiley, Williams and Wilkens, KTO, etc., issued backfiles of many scientific and other serial titles on microform. Almost without exception, these offerings consisted of periodical runs on microfilm until Johnson Associates began offering microfiche editions of magazines. Where previously, continuous issues of periodicals appeared on microfilm rolls, cartridges, or cassettes, now one issue of a magazine could be filmed and presented as a distinct physical and bibliographic entity. The unitization afforded by microfiche and the relative ease of operating the corresponding viewers (in sharp contrast to the difficulty-of-use encountered with many microfilm reading devices) convinced

Bell and Howell, Microcard Editions, and Microfilming Corporation of America to follow Johnson's lead. Soon several hundred general and scholarly periodicals on fiche offered librarians an alternative to the microfilm backfiles that for so long had dominated micropublishing of serials. Many libraries reported less user resistance to periodicals on fiche, and fiche was attractive as well for economic reasons summarized by one public librarian:

1. Microfiche is cheaper than cartridge contained roll film.
2. Fiche requires 2/10 of the space taken up by roll film.
3. Access is faster when data is stored on fiche.
4. Fiche viewers are generally less expensive than roll film viewers.
5. Production of fiche requires less time than production of roll film.[12]

In fact the growing interest in this medium prompted efforts to sustain original serial publishing in fiche, something that had not been attempted with microfilm. A highly specialized journal, *Wildlife Disease,* started in 1959, was published solely on fiche and in color beginning in 1972. The *International Microfilm Journal of Legal Medicine* has been published in fiche and film since 1965. Microforms International marketing Corporation (MIMC) experimented with a fiche edition of the abstract journal *International Abstracts of Biological Sciences* in 1970, but only one subscription order was received and the venture was dropped. MIMC tried again a year later, this time offering one hundred basic research journals on a simultaneous microfiche and paper release. To encourage participation by libraries the publisher permitted unlimited copyrights on the fiche edition for internal use only, this at a time when copyright was bcoming a bone of contention for publishers and librarians. Again response was lukewarm, and the simultaneous fiche release succumbed. The *American Journal of Computational Linguistics,* started in 1974, printed every article on a separate fiche which was accompanied by a summary card. And the *Journal of Modern History* began publishing some articles in 1976 in condensed form, with full text available in microform.

While original publishing in fiche languished in the United

States, Europe was successfully pushing ahead with programs that had not even reached the experimentation stage in American libraries. In France, where a century before Dagron had experimented with microphotography, the research library at Ugine Kuhlmann Chemical Complex began producing microfiche duplicates of the many scientific journals to which it subscribed. The silver halide master copy was used to reproduce additional copies on a diazo duplicator, and the copies were distributed to appropriate scientists or researchers who were interested in specific subject articles or entire journals.[13] The services of National de la Recherche Scientifique (CNRS) in Paris were even more extensive. This center offered subscriptions to no fewer than 15,000 international journals, edited and collated by subject for distribution to interested scientists. Very few journals were offered in their entirety.

Photocopy machines already were in use on a wide scale in libraries and industrial concerns where either copies or issues of periodicals were reproduced for interested users. When CNRS began its microfiche service, the cost of reproducing twenty pages of a paper journal on a photocopy machine was approximately one dollar. However, a microfiche copy could be made for only five cents or less. In fact, one entire fiche of 98 frames or pages cost only five cents. And, if the reader desired page copy, a reader/printer would produce paper copy for about another five cents.

The crucial factor here was the development of fast, inexpensive microfiche duplication, making reproduction of entire journals possible as quickly as with photocopy machines and at less cost.

The Williams and Wilkins Company was not the only publisher to look at such widespread microform and photocopy reproduction with a jaundiced eye, but no other firm made such an aggressive stand in favor of publisher and author rights. Williams and Wilkins brought suit against the National Institute of Health and the National Library of Medicine for what the company claimed was widespread, illegal photocopying of medical journal articles. In February of 1972 Commissioner Davis of the U.S. Court of Claims handed down a decision finding that the Williams and Wilkins Company was "entitled to recover reasonable and entire compensation for infringement of copyright" by the defendant's libraries who "operate comprehensive duplication systems which provide every year thousands of photocopies of articles, many of which are copies of the same article."

The consternation this decision produced in the library community was short-lived, however, as the U.S. Circuit Court of Appeals overturned the Court of Claims decision, ruling that photocopying of medical journal articles by government library defendants was fair use. The case ultimately made its way to the U.S. Supreme Court where, in 1975, the justices deadlocked 4–4 on the Williams and Wilkins suit, thereby upholding the libraries' victory in the U.S. Circuit Court of Appeals.

Only a year later, the Congress of the United States passed a comprehensive revision of the copyright law, including guidelines recommended by an *ad hoc* group of education associations, librarians, publishers, and authors. The guidelines allowed teachers or researchers to make a single copy of a chapter from a book, a short story or a poem, an article from a newspaper or periodical, etc., if needed for professional work. Libraries were allowed to continue interlibrary loan by copying the following: Out-of-print works unobtainable at a fair price, published works for purposes of replacement of damaged copies, unpublished works for preservation and security, up to six copies a year of small excerpts from long works, and up to six copies a year of any periodical published within the last five years.

Faced with ubiquitous copyright infringement (photocopying and microform distribution), publishers at the same time were being urged to convert scientific and technical journals to inexpensive microform originals as a method of making specialized journals attractive to a wider audience. Warren Bovee, a professor of journalism at Marquette University, earlier appealed to editors to recognize the potential benefits of fiche for readers and publishers alike.[14] He reminded them that, because of press and paper sizes, the number of pages in a periodical is usually a multiple of eight. If an editor has enough material to publish 59 pages, he usually is compelled to either eliminate three pages or add another five. Not so with fiche! On a standard 98 frame fiche, any number of pages up to 98 can be included and if some blank pages are left they pose no large problems to the editor who would despair at seeing blank pages in a paper journal. Long bibliographies, technical notes, and diagrams once excluded for lack of space could be provided to readers at no extra cost. Continuous line illustrations and four-color reproductions, so expensive that they usually are the exclusive domain of magazines of the coffee table variety, become eminently practical for the fiche publisher. No screening or engraving is needed to prepare photographs for fiche reproduction, ergo 98 full page photographs are as inexpensive as 98 pages of print. Full color magazines on fiche are no burden to the publisher, especially to the publisher of smaller circulation journals. In fact, only when a magazine is near or above 50,000 subscribers does printing paper stock become as inexpensive as producing microfiche. Since only 10 percent of the scientific and technical journals listed in the Standard Periodical Directory have circulations above 50,000, the potential savings available to publishers who stock the shelves of libraries are enormous. A monthly journal with a circulation of10,0000 could save about $25,000 a year by publishing with microfiche. When half-tones are used, the economic advantage of fiche increases. With a journal of 4,000 circulation, color microfiche, by Bovee's estimate, cost no more than black and white printing. This calculation was based on a journal with only ten photographs in color. Printing costs would rise astronomically if more color separations were used throughout the paper edition, but the microfiche costs for that journal would remain the same. The price of color fiche remains the same, whether color is used once or on all 96 pages.

Summarizing the economic perils of scholarly publishing, Bovee warned that editors of scientific and technical journals should, at a minimum, provide a printed and a concurrent, inexpensive microfiche version of these publications. "For scholars, the alternative has long been publish or perish. For publishers, it may soon become microfiche or perish."

Undaunted by past failures, MIMC in 1975 once again showed the flag with a fiche version of the weekly organic chemistry journal *Tetrahedron Letters*. Hardcopy and fiche editions of this journal were published simultaneously, but the fiche version was offered free to some five hundred institutional subscribers. The printed version had over 5,000 subscribers, at a subscription rate of over $200.00 per year. After an introductory test period, MIMC started charging $160.00 per year for the fiche version alone, and $100.00 per year for the fiche supplement to the printed subscription.

In the same year, the American Chemical Society offered simultaneous microfiche releases of its sixteen journals; however, the Society offered the fiche as a separate subscription. Readers were to opt for one or the other, with paper and fiche versions selling for identical prices.

Another innovative program was started by the American Institute of Physics (AIP). Its "Current Physics Microform" was an offer of twenty-four primary journals on 16mm microfilm, cartridges or reels. Each month, subscribers received current editions of journals published by AIP with a printed table of contents accompanying the microfilm. Also, a printed cumulative index was provided with each month's issues with each monthly index cumulating all issues previously published in that subscription year. Subscribers were granted the right to make unlimited printed copies from the microform articles for internal use, and the total cost of the microform package was approximately twenty-five percent less than the price of the same subscriptions in paper.

A few publishers of individual journals also experimented with simultaneous microfiche releases (e.g., *Saturday Review/World, Microform Review, The Journal of Micrographics*), but the expectations voiced by Bovee and others were slow to materialize. Some publishers were concerned about loss of revenue, as evidenced by an editorial in an industry bulletin:

> No doubt a microform edition, realistically priced in relation to its low production and distribution costs would undercut the price of the paper edition to a point where the resultant decline in the circulation of the latter would widen the gap thus transferring even further sales to the micro edition with the demise of the paper edition the only ultimate solution . . . publishers must decide what they are selling—information or paper?[15]

This, despite Bovee's evidence that even partial conversion to microform would aid publishers. Others worried about the "chicken and egg syndrome" or whether publishers would be able to market large numbers of microforms to an audience, personal and institutional, which was ill prepared with suitable reading devices or the inclination to use them properly if available. How, they argued, could microforms be widely disseminated if no reasonably acceptable, low-cost readers were as available or as widespread in the office or home as the common typewriter? And yet, what impetus was there for individuals to invest in such a reader when so few materials were marketed in microform? Any number of excellent, large model readers was available to institutions, but small, portable reading devices were plagued by the same concerns voiced as early as 1966 in the "Psychophysical Aspects of Microimage Reading."

> In the normal reading situation, the primary concern normally relates to the ability of the individual to perform a specific reading task successfully rather than to physical ease in reading. In the case of the microimage, however, we are conerned with very subtle conditions that are likely to prejudice persons against microimage reading. Such conditions involve petty annoyances and the slow onset of fatigue often associated with use of improperly designed microimage reading equipment. If microimage reading for pleasure is to be accepted by the general public, these shortcomings of present equipment must be overcome.[16]

These shortcomings of portable readers are still with us, as anyone who has recently struggled with small, inexpensive viewing devices can testify. Users are extremely sensitive to image sharpness, and unsatisfactory resolution rivals mutilated issues as a cause of migraine in otherwise contented library patrons.

Fiche are afflicted with other problems associated with microforms in general. In addition to the complaints about unsatisfactory viewing equipment, there are the difficulties of comparing different texts or making notes on microforms, of equipping and staffing a microtexts reading area, of providing for equipment and file maintenance and security (particularly with fiche), and of learning to cope with the generic problem labelled "user resistance." (Figure 11) Of all the issues, the latter complaint is probably the least valid. User resistance, as Francis Spreitzer discovered in a remarkably underpublicized study of microform systems in the United States, is more frequently "librarian resistance."[17] Spreitzer found that "patron resistance to using microforms was due largely to librarians who discourage use by sticking the files and equipment in inconvenient areas of

Figure 11

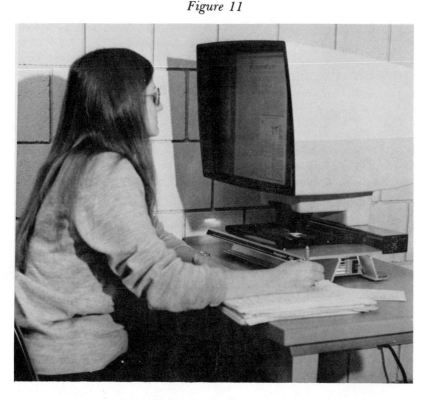

the library, allowing the equipment to break down, providing inadequate light and writing space in the microform area or not telling patrons microforms are available . . . The problem did not lie with patrons having trouble operating the equipment as librarians like to believe." In rating the microform facilities in libraries he visited, Spreitzer called 33 percent very bad, 10 percent good, and the majority "barely acceptable."

The negative factors of microform cannot be ignored. They are highly visible and substantial. However, in any cost comparison of paper and microforms, "the evidence indicates that substantial savings accrue when current paper periodicals are replaced with commercially available microform reproductions.[18]

When considering the advantages and disadvantages of microforms, the final argument seems always to settle on costs. Despite dissatisfaction with readers and methods of use, libraries are relying more and more on microforms because the costs of obtaining and maintaining many materials on microform is considerably less expensive than paper. This is especially true with periodical backfiles, which are generally much more expensive (particularly in reprint) than microform editions. Low cost, ease of replacement, and economical storage are strong arguments in favor of serials in microform.

NOTES

1. Osborne, Andrew D. *Serial Publications* (Chicago: American Libirary Association, 1973), p. 434

2. *Report of the New York Public Library of 1939* (New York, 1940), p. 63.

3. Weiss, Dudley A. "Maintenance of Materials Survey," *Library Binder* 17 : 9–11.

4. Brown, Norman. "Price Indexes for 76," *Library Journal* 101 (August 1976): 1600–1605.

5. Blair, Stewart. "Periodicals and the Liberal Arts College,"*College and Research Libraries* (September 1975) pp. 371–378.

6. Williams, Gordon. *Background and Proposal for a National Lending Library for Journals* (Chicago: Center for Research Libraries, n.d.) p. 36.

7. Wood, D.A. et al. "Investigation of the Cost of Periodical Replacement in the Periodical Reading Room of the University Library," in *Case Studies in Systems Analyses in a University Library*, (Scarecrow, 1968), p. 120–127.

8. Hendrick, Clyde and Murfin, Marjorie. "Project Library Ripoff: A Study of Periodical Mutilation in a University Library," *College and Research Libraries* (November 1974) pp. 402–411.

9. Gore, Daniel. "Zero Growth: When is not Enough?" *The Journal of Academic Librarianship* (November 1975) pp. 4–5.

10. Rider, Fremont. *Scholar and the Future of the Research Library* (Hadham Press, 1944).

11. Metcalf, Keyes D. *Planning Academic and Research Library Buildings*. New York: McGraw Hill 1965.

12. Fischer, Mary L. "The Use of COM at Los Angeles Public Library," *The Journal of Micrographics* 6 (May 1973): 205–210.

13. Gray, Edward. "Subscriptions on Microfiche: An Irreversible Trend," *Journal of Micrographics* 8 (May 1975): 241–244.

14. Bovee, Waren G. "Scientific and Technical Journals on Microfiche," *IEEE Transactions on Professional Communications* September 1973, pp. 113–116.

15. "The Paradox of Microduplications" an editorial, *The NCC d Bulletin.* 2 (Summer 1969): 1.

16. Ullrich, O.A. and Walkup, Lewis E. "Psychophysical Aspects of Micro-image Reading," *Battelle Technical Review* (January 1966), pp. 10–14.

17. "Spreitzer Criticizes Librarians' Attitude toward Microforms," *Advanced Technology Libraries.* October 1975, p.1.

18. Reed, Jutta R. "Cost Comparison of Periodicals in Hard/Copy and on Microforms," *Microform Review* July, 1976, pp. 185–190.

Chapter 5

Monographs in Microform

Monographic collections have been merchandized by micro-publishers in numbers approaching those of periodicals and government publications, but only recently has original publishing in microform been attempted by publishers of scholarly books. It was Norman Mangouni, of the State University of New York, who claimed first publishing of an original monograph on microfiche (1972) for his press,[1] an experiment forcibly imposed by the financial perils besetting scholarly publishing outlined by one panel of experts:

> The reasons for the present troubled situation are clear. University presses are non-profit institutions that exist largely to publish specialized scholarly works that are not publishable commercially. Thus they tend to be on the fringe of solvency at best—dependent on subsidies, trying to break even on small editions at low prices, issuing esoteric books for readers who use them primarily in libraries as subsidies come mainly from universities, and the chief customers are university and public libraries. But American universities, both public and private, have severe financial difficulties today; budgets are being drastically cut, and among the first to be cut are the subsidies for university presses since the presses are not directly involved with undergraduate teaching. At the same time, the budgets of university libraries are also being cut, or being held level. Even the latter means less money for books, since the operating expenses of libraries keep increasing. In addition—and this is a very important factor—U.S. federal appropriations for libraries have been cut from $25 million in 1969 to $11 million in 1972. Meanwhile the costs of every aspect of publishing—printing, advertising, postage, warehousing, and so forth have been increasing under inflationary pressure. Costs have risen while the market has shrunk, and while subsidies have been or are threatened to be cut.[2]

Squeezed by rising costs and declining markets, scholarly presses began cutting back production of general titles and spurned altogether those esoteric works of extreme length that once flowed smoothly onto library shelves. The ensuing clamor from academic writers, particularly those young scholars whose careers depended upon publications, worked to ameliorate the disdain microforms customarily elicited from professional ranks. Scholars were admonished to:

> regard as more respectable than we have forms of publication other than the traditionally manufactured book or monograph. Publication by means of microfilm, microfiche, etc., may be the only means by which works with limited audience appeal can be produced under current market conditions. The number of reprint series via microfilm is increasing and might well be paralleled by microfilm series of original works.[3]

Some publishers were skeptical. They examined the costs of producing finished books—royalties, editing, printing, binding, marketing—and found that micropublishing would change only the production of individual copies, substituting micro-images for the printing, paper, binding and jacketing. Of all costs, printing, paper, and binding comprise only fifteen to twenty percent of the retail price of a finished book. The bulk of expense is the editorial and compositional crafts of creating a viable manuscirpt. Then, too, the printing costs that are subject to reduction with microform also decline drastically in long runs of conventional paper editions, especially with paperbacks where the per copy cost of printing and binding mass market paperbacks can fall below the price of reproducing the same edition in microfiche.

The argument was continued on the grounds that the low prices of many microform collections were not a direct result of economies afforded by micrographic reproduction but, instead, were a result of the presence in the public domain of much micropublished material; hence, royalties and editing costs were virtually nonexistent. Another contributing factor to low prices was the usual offerings of large periodical sets or other collections whose marketing costs fell far below those of individual monographs.

The performance of one major scholarly publisher—the University of Toronto Press—seemed to buttress the contention that prices of original monogrpahs in fiche would have to be equal to or even higher than conventional books. Toronto, one of the earliest presses to experiment with fiche editions, did price its fiche copies at the same level as simultaneous conventional editions. But unlike serials, where the purchase of microform editions at comparable prices to paper copies still afforded considerable savings in binding, fiche monographs offered at no reduction in price provided very little incentive for purchase by librarians.

But wait, there is more! In the dock are other witnesses, and their testimony opens a window of doubt on what may have seemed to be a closed case. While the overhead costs of editing and marketing do remain fixed, whatever the publishing medium, production costs of microform editions may be only a small percentage of the costs of composing, printing and binding a paper book.[4] Publishers of printed books must decide on the number of copies to be issued, and they must contract for all of the copies at once if the economies of edition printing are to be realized. Publishers then stock copies and sell them off the shelf as orders come in. Anticipating demand of the market in advance is as challenging as trying to sell a microfilm camera to a commercial bindery. In the paperback market, for example, for every copy placed in a customer's hands another copy may be returned to the publisher unsold. This evil the micropublisher successfully avoids. "On demand micropublishing," the production of copies subsequent to receipt of orders, takes the element of risk out of most microform publishing endeavors. Only a very, very few attempts have been made by micropublishers to create materials for the academic market in advance of sales.[5] Micropublishers do not make a copy until an order is received, and the duplication process is a straight-line cost where each duplicate costs the same as every other duplicate copy no matter now many are produced. No need exists to maintain inventory stock, and the micropublications always are in-print. Micropublishing of monographs is a faster and more economical method of book production. The microform edition brings an author's work to an audience with greater speed, its mailing and distribution expenses are much lower, and price and storage space savings may be enjoyed by institutional customers.

The University Presses of Toronto, Washington, Southern Illinois, Kansas, Texas, Chicago, and New York have experimented with simultaneous and/or original microfiche editions. Unfortunately, prices of simultaneous fiche editions typically were comparable to hard copy charges and customer response was disappointing.[6] in 1976, however, the University of Chicago Press pioneered a "Text/Fiche" approach that may eventually prove to be the most adaptable form of original micropublication of monographs. Chicago Press issued printed and bound texts accompanied by pictorial microfiche in full color or black and white. The texts were structured in two parts—introductory material running into a score or more pages, followed by a caption list locating and identifying all images on the fiche.

For short run productions, the "Text/Fiche" method permitted inclusion of extremely numerous full color photographs, as in the edition of "Persepolis in Ancient Iran" which contained 1,000 photographs and just 57 pages of text and sold for $25,000 per copy. Even more important was the vast superiority of color fiche which, unlike printed images, provided fidelity of tonal ranges and exact colors.[7]

Another significant potential for "Text/Fiche" lies in the bringing together of many museum collections into one co-operative, economic publication with color reproductions of exceedingly impressive quality. Such ventures would greatly expand the publishing activites of many museums which cannot now afford expensive printed editions. Since museums typically show only a small percentage of their treasures at any one time, much material owned by museums is rarely, if ever, seen by the public. Microfiche can open doors for a much larger audience to enjoy cultural treasures that may not otherwise be available.

Hounded by rising costs and dwindling markets, scholarly presses have experimented with microforms only to discover less than anticipated economies of production and a lukewarm audience without the widespread private means to utilize micro-form editions. As was true of original serials in microform, publishers are skeptical of succeeding in a market whose foundation balances on a reader screen especially when so few private individuals possess the means to peruse micropublications. And yet, what motivation does an individual have to purchase reading equipment when so little original material is available in microform?

It therefore comes as no surprise that only a few original

works have been published in microeditions, yet hordes of collections (many in the public domain) have been snatched up by micropublishers and sold to institutional purchasers who secure the necessary reading devices. Here, all sides benefit: the micropublisher reaps the fruits of his labor; the library secures convenient-to-acquire research collections that are far less expensive than the originals, if in fact the originals are available; and the researcher obtains necessary sources of information whose access, without microform, would typically be delayed by interlibrary loans or simply be denied altogether.

An attempt will be made in the following pages to survey large monographic collections that have been gathered by micropublishers and made availble to libraries. In part, the listing is illustrative, and no claim of comprehensiveness is made or implied.

The number and variety of microform collections is stupendous, and collections of fewer than 1,000 discrete entries are excluded from the following pages as are documents or collections of individual associations or societies and materials by or about solitary individuals. The arbitrary decision to exclude certain types of material was done in support of brevity and general interest. It should be noted that, while many indexes are included in the stated prices of collections, some are priced separately. And when catalog cards are offered, they are almost always sold separately. Every attempt has been made to apply accurate and judicious descriptions of various micropublisher endeavors, and the authors apologize for any omissions or inaccuracies in summaries of the following collections of primarily monographic literature.

Selected Americana from Sabin's Dictionary of Books Relating to Americana from Its Discovery to the Present Time

Entries from Sabin that relate to the Americas and are textually significant with primary emphasis on North America. Many translations and subsequent editions are omitted.

Index: Catalog cards are provided with the collection

Publisher and form: Lost Cause Press—Microfiche

Anti-Slavery Propaganda in the Oberlin College Library

American anti-slavery propaganda published before January, 1863, and a smaller gathering of pro-slavery literature and British anti-slavery propaganda.

Index: Catalog cards are provided

Publisher and form: Lost Cause Press—Microfiche

Center for Alcohol Studies, Rutgers University. Raymond G. McCarthy Memorial Collection of Alcohol Literature

Nearly 20,000 documents from the Center of Alcohol Studies, Rutgers University, dealing with alcohol and alcoholism. The documents were drawn from many academic disciplines and professional or vocational fields, e.g., biochemistry, psychology, law, education, police science, theology, medicine, economics, public health. The original may be an article in a scientific journal, a chapter in a book, a dissertation, or a report in a conference proceeding. It may deal with any society or time period, and may be in a variety of languages.

Index: International Bibliography of Studies on Alcohol.

Publisher and form: Johnson Associates—Microfiche

Goldsmiths'–Kress Library of Economic Literature

Consisting of the combined holdings of two libraries unrivalled for their superb collections of early works in the literature of business and economics: The Goldsmiths' Library at the University of London and the Kress Library at Harvard. Available in two segments, Segment 1, *Printed Books through 1800,* and Segment 2, *Printed Books, 1808–1850.*

Index: A Consolidated Guide. Catalog cards also are available.

Publisher and form: Research Publications—Microfilm

Black Culture Collection

Rare books, pamphlets, papers, and other miscellaneous documents from Atlanta University's Trevor–Arnett Library, one of the leading centers of African and African–American research material in the world.

Index: Book catalog of subjects, authors, and titles.

Publisher and form: Bell and Howell—Microfilm

Documents on Contemporary China 1949–1975

A collection of some 3400 items in the field of Social Science drawn from the libraries of Columbia University, and comprising material on Chinese party and government, economic data, biographies, Red Guard translations, and research and analysis reports. Almost all items are translated into English.

Index: Bibliographic listing and author and subject indexes

Publisher and form: Johnson Associates—Microfiche

JSAS: Catalog of Selected Documents in Psychology Microfiche Collection

Original psychology material from technical reports, bibliographies, teaching materials, lectures, literature reviews, discussions, experimental studies, task force reports, projects in progress, etc. All inclusions are original material published only in microfiche.

Index: JSAS: Catalog of Selected Documents in Psychology

Publisher and form: Johnson Associates—Microfiche

Early English Books, 1475-1640

An ongoing project to film the works listed in Pollard and Redgraves's "A Short Title Catalogue of Books, 1475–1640. About 17,000 titles are filmed already, with approximately 100,000 pages added each year.

Index: Early English Books, 1475–1640. A Partial List by STC Numbers. Cross Index by STC Numbers.

Publisher and form: University Microfilms International— Microfilm

Early English Books, 1641-1700

Ongoing project to film the books listed in the "Short Title Catalogue of Books Printed in England, Scotland, Ireland, Wales, and British America and of English Books Printed in other Countries, 1641–1700," by Donald Wing. About 100,000 pages are added each year.

Index: English Books, 1641–1700, a Partial list by Wing Numbers.

Publisher and form: Univeristy Microfilms International— Microfilm

Early American Imprints, First Series (Evans) 1639-1800; and Second Series (Shaw-Shoemaker) 1801-1819

Approximately 42,000 non-serials titles published in the United States from 1639–1800 and listed in the "American Bibliography, Chronological Dictionary of all Books, Pamphlets, and Periodical Publications Printed in the United States of America from the Genesis of Printing in 1639 Down to and Including the year 1820" by Charles Evans; and the 50,000 non-serial titles published in the United States from 1801–1819 and listed in the "American Bibliogrpahy; A preliminary Check List for 1801–1819" by Ralph Shaw and Richard Shoemaker.

Index: Volume 14 of "American Bibliography . . ." and volume 22 of "American Bibliography, A Preliminary Checklist . . ."

Publisher and form: Readex—Microprint

American Culture Series I and II

Series I is a collection of 250 rare titles published between 1493 and 1806, providing a broad survey of American government, printing, literature, history, etc. Series II emphasizes the period 1801–75. When completed, the series will include more than 6,000 titles.

Index: No index, but guides are available from the publisher.

Publisher and form: University Microfilms International— Microfilm

PCMI Library Collections

Five series covering American Civilization, Literature–Humanities, Social Sciences, Science and Technology, and Government Documents. Each of the books filmed for these collections was cited in at least two standard subject bibliographies. Each year about 700 volumes (300,000 pages) of additional material is made available.

Index: A full set of Library of Congress Catalog cards is included in the price of each collection.

Publisher and form: National Cash Register Company— Ultra-high Microfiche (120×)

Library of American Civilization

A collection of about 15,000 titles about the United States and American life from the beginning to 1914, primarily composed of monographs but including 62 periodicals and some pamphlets and government documents.

Index: Author, title, subject and topical indexes in both book form and fiche are provided with the collection. Catalog cards are available for separate purchase.

Publisher and form: Library Resources, Inc.—Very high Microfiche (90×)

Landmarks of Science

An ongoing project encompassing 20,000 separate scientific publications specifically pertaining to the history of science. Most of the collection will be monographic; however, the relevant periodical literature is included.

Index: When the project is completed, a volume indexing subjects, authors, titles, editions, geographical area, and chronological period will be issued.

Publisher and form: Readex—Microprint

Afro–American Studies Materials

About 5,000 volumes documenting the social, political, and economic history of the Afro–American.

Index: Catalog cards are provided. A checklist of all materials in the collection also is available.

Publisher and form: Lost Cause Press—Microfiche

Spanish Drama of the Golden Age

The Comedia Collection from the University of Pennsylvania libraries of more than 3,200 plays of the

Spanish Golden Age, seventeenth through early nineteenth centuries.

Index: Author and title indexes

Publisher and form: Research Publications—Microfilm

Indians of the Americas

Extensive series of Indian Rights Association Papers, Smithsonian Institution bulletins and reports, monographs, and periodicals relating to the American Indian.

Index: Guides and indexes

Publisher and form: Microfilming Corporation of America
—Microfilm

Sotheby Catalog Series

A gathering of Sotheby Parke–Bernet sales catalogues annotated with prices and names of buyers, dating from 1734–1970.

Index: Guides with entries arranged in chronological order
as items appear on film.

Publisher and form: University Microfilms International—
Microfilm

American Labor Unions' Constitutions and Proceedings 1836–1974

History in original source documents of more than ninety American labor unions. Annual update service is available to provide continuing material on active unions.

Index: Keyword index and catalog cards

Publisher and form: Microfilming Corporation of America
—Microfilm

Women's History Research Center Collections on Microfilm

"Herstory," "Women and Health/Mental Health," and "Women and Law" are three units of diverse material documenting the past and contemporary history of women and the women's movement.

Index: Reel Guide

Publisher and form: Research Publications—Microfilm

Bibliography of American Women

Entries from the "Bibliography" by Dr. H. Carleton Marlow include monographic material written by and about women to 1904, containing some 50,000 printed books and titles.

Index: None

Publisher and form: Research Publications—Microfilm

History of Women

12,000 volumes mainly of printed books, but also including pamphlets and large series of periodicals covering the years 1487 through 1920 from the libraries of Radcliffe College, Smith College, Scripps College, etc. About seventy-five percent of the material is English language. The rest is in Western European languages.

Index: Bibliographic guide and catalog cards

Publisher and form: Research Publications—Microfilm

Western Americana

Frontier history of the Trans-Mississippi West, 1550–1900 from the libraries of Yale and the Newberry Library. More than 7,000 titles containing basic printed sources for the history of the discovery, exploration, settlement, and development of much of North America.

Index: Bibliographic guides and subject index and catalog cards

Publisher and form: Research Publications—Microfilm

Gerritsen Collection of Women's History (1543–1945)

More than 4,000 monographs, periodicals, and pamphlets recording the intellectual, political, and social history of women. Focus of much of the collection is on the history of American and British women, but there is substantial material from France, Germany and other European countries.

Index: Guide, indexes, and catalog cards

Publisher and form: Microfilming Corporation of America —Microfilm

Radical Pamphlet Literature: A Collection from the Taminment Library 1817–1970

Pamphlets reflecting the views of the Socialist Labor Party, Socialist Party, Communist Party, and many other radical left wing groups. Some of the subjects covered include trade unionism, anti-semitism, McCarthy era, women and blacks, civil rights, and writings of prominent revolutionaries.

Index: Guide to Collection

Publisher and form: Microfilming Corporation of America —Microfilm

Right Wing Collection of the University of Iowa Libraries

Periodicals, newsletters, pamphlets, flyers, broadsides, and various other ephemera from many parts of the United States focusing on right wing and conservative ideologies, including some libertarian material. Most material is from 1950 on, with scattered material from the 1920s.

Index: Guide and catalog cards

Publisher and form: Microfilming Corporation of America
—Microfilm

Human Relations Area Files

Ongoing series of primary sources on human behavior, social life, and culture on a world-wide basis. Contains a large number of manuscripts and periodical articles, as well as monographs.

Index: The Outline of World Cultures indexes area or culture. The Outline of Cultural Materials is a subject index. The HRAF Source Bibliography lists the holdings in the collection.

Publisher and form: Human Relations Area Files—
Microfiche

University Microfilms International—
Microfilm

American Prose Fiction 1774–1900

11,000 titles from Lyle H. Wright's bibliographies of American fiction. All works appear in sequence alphabetically by order or, if anonymous, by title as in the Wright bibliographies.

Index: Catalog cards are supplied for each title. Author and reel guides are available

Publisher and form: *University Microfilms International—*
Microfilm

Lost Cause Press—Microfiche

Research Publications—Microfilm

Confederate Imprints

7,000 entries, books and miscellaneous publications of the Confederate States of America as listed in "Confederate Imprints, A Check List" by Marjorie Lyle Crandall and "More Confederate Imprints" by Richard Harwell.

Index: Bibliographies and reel guides

Publisher and form: Research Publications—Microfilm

American Poetry 1609–1900

Nearly 300 years of American verse—the work of major and minor poets, the doggerel and poor and pious poetry of obscure poets, and the poetical works of prose writers like Thoreau, Melville, and Hawthorne —from the Brown University Library.

Index: Reel guides and catalog cards

Publisher and form: Research Publications—Microfilm

New York Times Oral History Program

Various library collections of the American Indian's view of his history, civil rights movement, growth of labor unions, film history, Chinese History, Contemporary Jewry, etc.

Index: Various indexing

Publisher and form: Microfilming Corporation of America
—Microfiche and film

American Autobiographies 1676–1900

A large compilation of works from Kaplan's *Bibliography of American Autobiographies* containing works about subjects who were born in the United States and who lived here or abroad and those who were born in foreign lands and emigrated to the United States.

Index: A partial subject index, shipping lists and catalog cards

Publisher and form: Northwest Micrographics—Microfiche

Crime and Juvenile Delinquency

More than two thousand titles from the library of the National Council of Crime and Delinquency covering crime by municipal, county, state, federal, and privately-generated documents published primarily within the past twenty-five years.

Index: Guide, subject index, and catalog cards

Publisher and form: Microfilming Corporation of America —Microfiche

NOTES

1. "SUNY Press and Microfiche," *Microform Review* 2 (July 1973): 166.
2. Bailey, Herbert S. Jr. et al., "The Impending Crisis in University Publishing," *Scholarly Publishing* 3(3) (April 1972): 195–207.
3. Eckhardt, Caroline and Smith, John. "Facts to Scholarly Publishing: Book Length Works in Literature," *Publications of the Modern Language Association* 89(2) (March 1974): 360–68.
4. Mangouni, Norman. "Micropublishing Among the University Presses," *Microform Review* 3 (October 1974): 250–253.
5. Block, Larry and Schmidt, Richard E. "Demand Publishing," *Journal of Micropublishing* 52 (November 1971): 81–82.
6. Montagnes, Ian. "Microfiche and the Scholarly Publisher," *Scholarly Publishing* 7 (October 1975): 63–84.
7. "Chicago Press Launches New Micropublishing Project: Text/Fiche," *Publishers Weekly* 209 (May 24, 1976): 40–43.

Chapter 6

Micrographics & Government Publications

No other sector of the American microform arena, neither business nor education, has adopted micrographics as eagerly or has contributed as much to continued development as the United States Government. The claim of Bernard Williams that the "largest primary publishing activity ever undertaken on microform (and possibly on any other medium) is that of the U.S. Government,"[1] has its roots in that early microfilming project of the National Recovery Administration and Agricultural Adjustment Agency in 1935 and is now conclusively demonstrated by the Government Printing Office's plan to distribute microfiche editions of publications to depository libraries. Between those events reside a number and variety of individual agency projects too formidable to describe within the scope of this work. Then, too, micropublishers have not been lax in their attention to library needs where documents are concerned. No other area of publishing endeavor compares with the coverage —sometimes with three or more companies issuing identical material—of census statistics, Congressional miscellania, judicial opinions, and assorted catalogs and indexes. The accessibility of documents and the peculiarities of copyright no doubt have much to do with micropublishing ventures in this field; nonetheless, their variety and size are astonishing. First, however, note the ambition of early internal Government projects.

The Clearinghouse for Scientific and Technical Information (COSATI), of the United States Department of Commerce, was directed to analyze and index in its *U.S. Government Research and Development Reports* unclassified documents prepared by the

Atomic Energy Commission (AEC), the National Aeronautics and Space Administration (NASA), assorted defense agencies, and many other departments and agencies of the federal government. COSATI published such documents in hard copy and—from 1964 on and at a reduced price—microfiche. The fiche was produced in an internal processing operation utilizing two step and repeat cameras capable of filming up to fifteen hundred pages per day.[2] Silver halide originals were duplicated onto diazo film which then became masters for third generation diazo dissemination copies. Hard copy was produced directly from finished microfiche on a step and repeat enlarger printer with a dry silver print-out process. In its first years of operation, COSATI's production of hard copy and microfiche made possible an annual dissemination of more than fifty thousand documents of substantial value to the scientific community.

In 1970, the name of the Clearninghouse was changed to National Technical Information Service (NTIS), and its charter was expanded to include all types of material of general interest reported by federal agencies, their contractors, or grantees.[3] Less than five years after its inception, NTIS had nearly one million reports on file and was disseminating three million reports each year. Of those three million documents, fully one-half were ordered in microfiche by NTIS customers.

A similar system in operation at the same date was originated by the U.S. Defense Documentation Center (DDC), which had the responsibility of providing industry with free information on the manifold aspects of government contracts. Contract-related material was available on microfiche, or hardcopy run from 35mm rolls on a XEROX "copyflo" and from microfiche on automatic step and repeat enlarger printers. With both forms of material provided free, there was no price incentive in favor of fiche, yet that format was selected by at least fifteen percent of the recipients. Like the AEC and NASA, DDC's reports were provided to the Clearinghouse for distribution to a wider audience. AEC and NASA, however, contracted with commercial vendors for the filming of their documents. AEC was sending eighty-five percent of its report literature in microfiche (some three million individual fiche) to AEC offices and labs, to contractors, and to other federal agencies and libraries. In the heyday of the space program, NASA was exploiting the attributes of microform to dispatch more than forty thousand documents annually to NASA installations world-wide. Speed of report preparation and dissemination was the critical factor here, as some eight million microfiche per year were distributed to scientists and engineers at work on NASA projects.[4]

An enormous microform service well known to librarians is the Educational Research Information Center (ERIC). ERIC was started in 1964 by the Office of Education, Department of Health, Education, and Welfare. The basic objective of ERIC was to provide reliable, current educational research and related information promptly and inexpensively to teachers, administrators, researchers,business, and the general public.[5] A number of specialized centers or clearinghouses were established throughout the Untied States where professional staffers reviewed literature to decide its value. Each center concentrated on specific educational topics. If a document was judged valuable to others, it was abstracted and indexed and relayed to a commercial vendor for microform and hard copy reproduction.

The growth of ERIC was phenomenal. Three years after its inception, ERIC sold more than one-half million research reports. By 1973, ERIC was selling twelve million reports on fiche alone. Today, ERIC is a vital information system combining the latest technology of microforms and computers. Many libraries perform on-line computer searches of the ERIC data base, thereby providing students and researchers with citations to relevant literature that can be provided on the spot through off-line printing devices.

Many other federal agencies use microforms in internal filing systems and for publication programs. The National Archives and Records Service provides basic documentation for research in history, economics, law, genealogy, and public administration. Since 1940, the National Archives has been filming records and documents to protect them against damage and destruction and to make copies available to libraries.[6] Some of the first documents to be filmed were official records of the Government including "Papers of the Continental Congress," "Territorial Papers," "State Department Registers of Correspondence," "Military Affairs," and "Federal Population Censuses." For those users interested in genealogy and family history, the population schedules are a mine of information. Historians use those records for studies of such subjects as westward expansion, population shifts, free and slave labor, regional history, and immigration.

Other material provided through the National Archives microfilm services ranges from the "Records of the Russian–American Company," information on the economic and political agent governing Alaska before its purchase by the United States in 1867, to "Records of Confederate Soldiers," containing all the names of Confederate Soldiers and their Service records. The National Archives sells many thousands of microfilm copies to interested researchers every year.

Another enormous convert to microfilm was the Library of Congress (LC). What began as a microfilm preservation program to protect material that was deteriorating or not suitable for rebinding gradually evolved into a large-scale system of information retrieval encompassing all manner of microforms. LC struggled to preserve thousands of newspapers from the far corners of the earth, and, as a result, ran head on into the problems of newspaper preservation. Beginning in 1939, LC microfilmed the *Washington Post, Washington Star,* and *National Intelligencer.* Obtaining favorable reactions to the project, the Library through the succeeding years continued to convert pulp paper newspapers to film—no small project, since a total of seventy-five million pages of newsprint were destined for conversion. (The newspaper files took up about eighteen linear miles of shelf space.)[7] At the present date, the Library's conversion program is somewhat more than half-way to completion.

Newspapers are not the only material in the Library to be converted to film. Since 1962, more than five thousand rare monographs have been filmed annually. When filming is completed, rare books can be placed on closed reserve and a microfilm positive print becomes user copy. The library strives to collect rare historical resources, and, over the years, has managed to film and preserve the early legislative records, statutory laws, court records, and constitutional records for the fifty states. The Copyright Office in LC receives nineteen different application forms from authors, composers, and publishers. These forms, plus the original documents, are microfilmed to ensure against loss. The card catalog of copyrighted works, containing eleven million records, is also retained on microfilm. The goal of filming all Presidential Papers owned by LC was recently completed after seventeen years of toil. Similar efforts to film Latin American and Southern Asia gazettes are ongoing. In all, LC's commitment to preservation of rare and deteriorating research material involves filming more than seven million pages each year and the continued preparation of distribution copies to all those who seek to utilize the Library's priceless collections.[8]

In breadth of micrographics experimentation and successful implementation, no branch of government exceeds the Defense Department. The Department of the Army alone built more than three thousand microform systems with a value of equipment estimated at over $100 million.[9] Successful applications of computer-output-microfilm are commonplace.

The State Department keeps employee medical records on microfilm, uses aperture cards for a newspaper clippings file, and furnishes a number of COM-produced reports. The Treasury Department has more than a million registration records relating to the National Firearms Act in an automated microform storage and retrieval unit, as well as millions upon millions of filmed bonds and similar documents. The Federal Bureau of Investigation keeps fingerprints and other data on microfilm; the Postal Service has a mcirofilm system for processing payrolls; the National Library of Medicine microfilms historic medical publications; the Internal Revenue microfilms tax accounts; and the Census Bureau employs film for population surveys and other reports. The Federal Aviation Agency distributes federal supply catalogs in fiche and internal COM-prepared reports are ubiquitous. The Securities and Exchange Commission (SEC), with a system named DISCLOSURE, prepares all financial information filed with the Government by private corporations. A few years ago the people who asked SEC for data on individual corporations could wait five or six weeks for a reply. Today annual reports, registration statements, and much else is available on microfiche in a few days or even hours.

Where color is important, conversion to microform has proved not to be an obstacle. The Department of Agriculture has color microfilm files of all meat and poultry labels retrievable by computer. The Federal Drug Administration's Bureau of Veterinary Medicine has 16mm color microfilm labels for new drug applications, and the U.S. Geological Survey is preparing 105mm color microfilm of maps so that orders for duplication can be run from film masters instead of perishable, original maps.

The inexorable expansion of micrographics continued as the Government Printing Office (GPO) polled depository libraries in 1974 on their preferences regarding microform and/or hard copy document distribution. The response was very favorable toward microforms, hence the GPO proceeded with a pilot project (the Code of Federal Regulations on fiche) and let a contract to XIDEX for filming of depository publications.

The enterprise and imagination evidenced in this résumé of federal micrographics is proof that bureaucracies need not be total swamps of indifference to new ideas. To foster greater coordination government agencies voluntarily created a Federal Government Micrographics Council to serve as a forum for exchange of professional and technical information on all aspects of micrographics. The Council strives to help establish management programs, standards, and guidelines and to develop training programs for technicians. The Council has, whenever possible, promulgated compatibility among microform systems and standardization of formats and reduction ratios. The Council also seeks to influence laws and federal regulations relating to microforms.

The altruistic efforts of this Council to encourage cooperation and standardization among producers of microforms deserve the thanks of all those who are interested in preserving the sanity of microform users. The Council's work could well provide a model for micropublishers to follow in their attempts to bring a rational consistency to the microforms marketplace.

In 1953, the Readex Microprint Company began selling a Microprint edition of United States Government Publications. The individual documents were assembled by the Superintendent of Documents in the order in which they appeared in the *Monthly Catalog of U.S. Government Publications* and were forwarded to the Library of Congress, which filmed the entries for Readex. The publications were available in two annual collections: *Non-Depository Publications* 1953 on; and *Depository Pub-*

lications 1956 on. The Microprint copies of all publications, year by year, were arranged by *Monthly Catalog* entry numbers, hence the *Catalog* was a direct index to both sets.

Libraries collecting government documents found the nondepository publications particularly valuable because of the difficulty of obtaining the often fugitive and ephemeral material in this category. Then, too, depository Microprint editions had their value since classification, maintenance, and accessing of paper documents posed unique problems for many libraries. An important feature of the Readex depository collection was its acceptance by the Superinendent of Documents as a substitute for the original depository items. Once the Microprint edition was on the shelf, libraries could discard paper copies. Readex also provided free sets of catalog cards containing abbreviated information in headings for all U.S. Government departments.

Another notable commercial micropublication of government publications was the *Checklist of US Public Documents 1781–1970* by the U.S. Historical Documents Institute, Inc., a firm which has contributed several outstanding indexing projects for libraries. This project, like so many to follow, combined source material in microform with hard copy indexes. The efficacy of this approach rested on the convenience of use and familiarity with book indexes, particularly when searching vast files of data inexpensively packaged on microform. The data in this case involved the shelf list holdings of the Government Printing Office's Public Documents Library in Washington, D.C. Its card catalogs arranged by Superintendent of Documents call numbers were provided on microfilm with comprehensive companion book indexes to provide access to the filmed entries. The five original book indexes were arranged by: Superintendent of Documents classification numbers of Government Author-Organizations, Departmental Keywords, Government Serial titles, and Master Keywords to Publication Issuing offices. Purchasers of the *Checklist* used it primarily for identifying and acquiring out-of-print government publications, and for verification and interlibrary loans.

Carrollton Press, affiliated with the U.S. Historical Documents Institute, followed with a *Cumulative Subject Guide to U.S. Government Bibliographies 1924–1973*, with an accompanying

Bibliography Masterfile Collection of microfiche. The seven volume hard copy subject index cited more than eighteen thousand bibliographies published as separate books and pamphlets and some twenty-two thousand additional bibliographies issued as parts of other U.S. publications. The subject entries in the index were identical to *Monthly Catalog* entries, and the provided data included titles, authors, compilers, pagination, size, LC card numbers, Superintendent of Documents classification numbers, ordering information, and depository symbols. The full text bibliographies available in fiche were arranged in the same sequence as entries in the *Subject Guide,* so readers could conveniently browse through many titles grouped under common subject headings.

Another large Carrollton collection, the *Declassified Documents Reference System,* contained secret material subsequently declassified under the Freedom of Information Act. In all, more than ten thousand previously designated TOP SECRET, SECRET, AND CONFIDENTIAL documents from intelligence agencies and other departments of the U.S. Government were indexed and abstracted in book format while the cited deocuments were provided on microfiche. This collection was available on retrospective and annual subscriptions. Material was not arranged by date of publication but by date of declassification. Entries were included as they became available, and most of the material covered the period after 1940. As might be expected, Defense, State Department, and CIA documents were heavily represented, and, for post World War II history, such sources were invaluable.

The *Transportation Masterfile, 1921–71* collection consisted of the U.S. Department of Transportation Library's reference sources. This consisted of some 700,000 abstracts and annotated references to the technical and non-technical periodical literature on all modes of transportation and were issued on three hundred 16mm reels or cartridges (35mm reels were available at a somewhat higher price). Access to the collection was provided by two hard copy bibliographies: "Transportation Serial Titles" and "Subject Headings in Transportation Masterfilm, 1921–71."

Information about the history and proceedings of the United States Congress is now more complete and readily available to libraries and researchers because of the file management attributes of microform.

One very extensive compilation on the Legislative Branch is the *Proceedings of the U.S. Congress—1789–1970* by the U.S. Historical Documents Institute. Another dual media set, the *Proceedings* combines 572 reels of microfilm and 110 hard copy indexes of the *Congressional Record* (1873–1970), *Congressional Globe* (1833–1873), *Register of Debates* (1824–1838), and *Annals of Congress* (1789–1824). This collection comprises an official narrative for the first 182 years of the history of the Congress of the U.S.

For a thorough overview of the day-to-day activities of Congress, the Congressional Information Service publishes an outstanding index and correlative *CIS Microfiche Library* of all Committee Hearings, Committee Prints, House and Senate Reports, House and Senate Documents, House and Senate Special Publications, Senate Executive Reports, and Senate Executive Documents. CIS also offers *Congressional Bills on Microfiche*—House and Senate Bills, Resolutions, and Public Laws. Individual segments are shipped by Congress number, with bills already filed in numerical sequence. The convenience savings in space with this fiche approach needs no further amplification for any documents librarian who has choked on a diet of paper bills from the Government Printing Office.

For libraries not satisfied with partial retrospective coverage of Congress, CIS offers the *Serial Set Index and Companion Microfiche Library 1789–1969*, encompassing the *American State Papers* and *Serial Set* publications of the 15th Congress through the 91st Congress. The material is available in four separate parts or as a complete package. The *Serial Set*, so called because all the Congressional journals, correspondence, reports, and statistical data comprising the Set are bound in volumes numbered serially from one onwards, contains some of the most important material in the early history of the Republic.

Readex Microprint Company was the first micropublisher to offer the *American State Papers* and the U.S. *Serial Set*, obtainable either in groups (by individual Congresses) or in total. The Readex Collections were, of course, available on opaque Microprint cards, the *American State Papers* also being available from Information Handling Services (formerly Microcard Editions).

U.S. Congressional *Committee Prints* are published on microfiche by Greenwood Press. Prints, usually prepared by committee staffs providing background for areas of committee interest or investigation, or particular views of congressmen, contain information not widely accessible in libraries. Greenwood's fiche package includes nearly 4,000 Prints beginning with the 61st Congress, and is accessed through a hard cover bibliography arranged primarily by committee. Greenwood also published *Congressional Hearings* on microfiche with correlative shelflists and indexes by subject, committee, and bill number. Shelflist and indexes are provided both on fiche and hard copy.

The Congressional Record (vol. 1, 1873–) is available on 35mm microfilm from Princeton Microfilm Corporation. All indexes, daily digests, and appendices are included. Information Handling Services publishes the *Record* (1949–) on microfiche. Micromedia Limited has another set of microfilm, and Bell and Howell offers (1964–) on fiche.

United States Statutes at Large, the complete transcripts of all Congressional bills that have become law from 1789 on, is published on microfiche by Information Handling Services.

A strong impetus to the growth of microforms was their potential for bringing rare and inaccessible research material to the eyes of students and researchers in almost any locale. Nowhere is this more readily apparent than with the publications of foreign governments and international organizations.

Canada is well represented by the micropublishing accomplishments of Micromedia Limited, whose collections of Canadian Government documents include sets of *Federal Documents, Parliamentary Committees, Statistics 1841–1975*, and *Provincial and Municipal Documents*. Micromedia publishes many other special collections on *Indian Studies, Education, Music, Urban Affairs, Women*, and other topics.

The United States Historical Documents Institute (USDI) publishes the *Canadian Parliamentary Proceedings and Sessional Papers* (1841–1970) in a dual media reference set containing the full texts of Journals, Debates, and Sessional Papers of both houses of Parliament on 703 reels of 35mm microfilm accessed by 128 hardcover indexes. USDI also publishes the *Canadian Library of Parliament Card Catalogues* (French and English language) on sixty reels of 35mm microfilm.

Great Britain is well represented by the efforts of several micropublishers. Readex Microprint publishes the *British House of Commons Sessional Papers,* eighteenth to twentieth centuries. Advertised as "the richest and most important collection of printed government records in existence in any country," the *Papers* cover a wide variety of subjects relating not only to the government of Britain but to all those countries achieving their independence from the Empire.

Some of the more important subjects in the "Twentieth Century" set are India, Africa, World Wars I and II, Education, Social Insurance, Elections, and Franchise for Women. Earlier years also included papers laid before the House and ordered printed by the House; printed papers laid before Commons by Royal command; all bills, accounts, and papers; reports from select committees and Royal commissions; and state papers. Subject indexes and numerical lists for bills, reports, papers and command papers are provided. Readex also publishes the complete collection dating from 1066, of Hansard's *Parliamentary Debates.*

The United States Historical Documents Institute publishes the complete holdings of Parliamentary and Non-Parliamentary publications deposited in the *Controller's Library of Her Majesty's Stationery Office, 1922–1972.* The twelve million pages in this collection are issued on 4,000 reels of 35mm microfilm and can be purchased as a complete set or in a variety of sub-sets. The whole is indexed in hard copy volumes in the *Cumulative Index to HMSO Catalogues of Publications, 1922–1972.*

Somerset House (Chadwyck–Healey Ltd.) publishes many series of British non-Parliamentary documents (hence not included in "Sessional Papers"): *Overseas Trade, Economic Surveys, Ministry of Agriculture, etc.* The sets are issued primarily on microfiche.

Previously unpublished research material from the British Foreign Office is available on *Russia: Correspondence 1781–1945,* and on *Japan: Correspondence 1856–1940,* from Scholarly Resources Inc.

For government documents of France and Germany, Information Handling Services offers the following on microfiche: for France, *Journal Officiel, Debats Parlementaries, Chambre des Deputes,* and *Journal Officiel;* and for Germany, the Reichstag

Verhandlungen des Reichstags 1867–1933, the German Confeder-
ation 1815–66 *Protokolle der deutschen Bundesvaesammlung,* and
the Prussia Landtag *Stenographische Berichte 1849–1933.* Bell and
Howell has *El Archivo De Hidalgo Del Parral,* official reports and
records documenting the Spanish Colonial Era of Northern
Mexico, 1631–1821, and Readex Microprint publishes *Russian
Historical Sources,* a research source for the study of Russia and
East European Cultures composed primarily of government
documents.

Also on microfiche is Information Handling Services' collection of the *Organization of American States* which is a complete
source of all official documents including all Spanish and English translations of multilateral, bilateral, and regional agreements; conventions, treaties, agreements and arrangements to
which the OAS is a party; and final acts of conferences and
meetings of the OAS. The microfiche collection can be used in
conjunction with the indexes prepared by the OAS.

League of Nations Documents and Serial Publications 1919–1946
on microfilm is offered by Research Publications, Inc. The five
types of documents in the collection are those circulated to the
Assembly, those circulated to the Council, Circular Letters from
the Secretary-General to the Member States, Documents and
minutes of the Permanent Mandates Commission, and other
documents received from the outside by the Secretariat. In addition, all serial and miscellaneous publications of the League
are available, with guide indexes.

United Nations Publications are published on fiche by UNIFO
Publishers, Ltd. Readex Microprint Corporation has *UN Documents and Official Records, 1946–,* available on micro-opaques.
The United Nations' publications office also issues microform
editions of Treaty Series, records of U.N. organizations, and
other materials.

Census and other statistical materials are emphasized by
many micropublishers. Chadwyck–Healey Ltd. publishes *European Official Statistical Serials on Microfiche,* individual national
compendiums for Belgium, France, Germany, Italy, Poland,
Sweden, and the USSR. Greenwood Press has the *Current National Statistical Compendiums* also on fiche, a total of more than
270 post–1970 sources from some 88 countries. Clearwater
Publishing Company offers *Import-Export Microtables* of the Or-

ganization for Economic Cooperation and Development on fiche, containing foreign trade data broken down by commodity categories. Research Publications, Inc., has *International Population Census Publications* for almost 300 countries on microfilm. Redgrave publishes *Western European Census Reports, 1960 Census Period* for 22 countries on microfiche. Greenwood Press can provide microfilm and microfiche editions of *United States Census Publications, 1820–1967*, covering vital statistics on population, agriculture, housing, transportation, construction, governments, and many other subjects. Research Publications has the *United States Decennial Census Publications, 1790–1970* on microfilm, as well as *1790–1940 United States Population and Non-Population Censuses*. And Kraus–Thomson issues *State Censuses* on microfiche, a complete gathering of all reports and selected footnotes in *State Censuses, An Annotated Bibliography of Censuses of Population Taken After the Year 1970 by States and Territories of the United States* by Henry Dubester. Accessible here is esoteric data unavailable in many federal censuses on topics like mining, railroad construction, militias, convicts, schools, personal names, and other sources dear to the genealogist's heart. Brookhaven Press publishes a similar fiche edition.

Libraries attempting to build collections of State Documents have been frustrated by frequently haphazard systems of bibliographic control and distribution in state publication offices. Where comprehensive checklists and depository library systems for documents exist, access to state publications can equal that of the program for federal documenrs. But unfortunately, the indexing and dissemination of state documents is generally inadequate. Several micropublishers have seen the opportunity and provided needed services in the areas of state publications. Information Handling Services publishes *State Publications on Microfiche* with a "Checklist of Current Publications" covering all fifty states, the Virgin Islands, and Puerto Rico. Extensive indexing allows access by state agency, author, subject, or date of coverage.

Research Publications offers microfilm subscription services to the *Official Publications of the State of New York,* and the *State of Illinois.* Documents are accessed through checklists and indexes of the respective state publication offices.

Brookhaven Press publishes *Minnesota Executive Documents,*

1860–1924 and *Wisconsin Public Documents, 1852–1914* on microfiche. Hardcopy guides are provided.

Session Laws of American States are available on current subscriptions from Information Handling Services on microfiche, and from Redgrave which offers pre-1900 material from states and territories on microfiche. These collections provide a source of all public, private, and local law. Subject indexes and checklists are available.

Kraus-Thomson (KTO Microform) publishes *State Reports on Correction and Punishment, Poverty, and Public Welfare Prior to 1930.* This fiche resource includes all known official serial reports for eleven major states with a corresponding set of printed Library of Congress main entry catalog cards (LC).

Research Publications offers in microfilm the *Pennsylvania County and Regional Histories* covering the span 1830–1919, and *Sources of Massachusetts Legal History,* a record of all the legislation enacted by the Massachusetts Bay Colony and the state for the years 1628–1839, as well as other collections of state atlases and histories.

Greenwood Press publishes the *Urban Documents Microfiche Collection,* a series of city and county publications indexed by subject and geographical area.

Micropublishing also permits the convenient gathering of state blue books and legislative manuals into single, easy-to-acquire collections. Northern Micrographics, Inc., publishes on fiche *State Blue Books, Industrial Directories, Legislative Manuals,* and *Statistical Reports.* These publications provide data on state internal organization, voting patterns, industrial and commercial resources, and other areas of interest.

Legal resources in microform are explored in an excellent guide by Henry P. Tseng.[10] A sample of some of the larger collections are *Publications of the Permanent Court of International Justice* in microfilm by Research Publications, Inc., and *U.S. Reports on Microfiche* (opinions and miscellaneous orders of the U.S. Supreme Court from 1887–) from Information Handling Services.

A cumbersome tool for libraries to use and maintain in paper is the *Official Gazette of the U.S. Patent Office.* Bell and Howell issues a 35mm microfilm set dating from 1872, while Reserach

Publications has a microfiche set datng from 1790. XEROX University Microfilms has a microfilm set, 1872–.

Another large microform collection of government publications include *Government Translations Microform,* a product of Database Publications which is processed by the *Joint Publication Research Service* (JPRS), and offers microfilm or fiche versions of the translations of documents from the USSR, China, Eastern Europe, South America, and other areas. Indexes by subject, author, and country of origin are available. Readex Microprint also publishes JPRS Reports on micro-opaques dating from 1958. Johnson Associates publishes *The Nixon Administration,* a fiche collection of documents concerning the events following the Watergate Break-in on June 17, 1972, through the U.S. vs Connally trial of March 1975. This collection of fiche containing the Senate Watergate Hearings, House Judiciary Committee proceedings, and much additional material is accompanied by subject, author, and title indexes.

Johnson Associates also publishes *Reform of Local Government Structures in the United States, 1945–71,* a fiche collection of documents relating to the structure and organization of local government in the U.S. A printed bibliography and subject/geographic index accompany the set. The Congressional Information Service provides an outstanding source of statistical data—the *American Statistics Index* and corresponding Microfiche Library of statistics on virtually any subject imaginable, all culled from U.S. Government Populations. And UPDATA Publications, Inc., has the *U.S. Bureau of Mines Collection* on microfiche—a compilation of the Bureau's bulletins, reports, yearbooks, and other papers for the years 1910–1969—and the *National Advisory Committee for Aeronautics Collection 1915–58.*

An indeterminate number of smaller projects also have been prepared by micropublishers. They offer fiche editions of AEC Reports, annual reports of Executive Departments, the Federal Register, State Labor Reports, City Directories, Reports of Special Commissions, Proceedings of Presidential Nominating Conventions. And two firms—Microfilming Corporation of America and Pergamon Press—publish a selection of current U.S. Government periodicals on microfiche. The latter firm publishes a simultaneous fiche edition of the U.S. National Library of Medicine's *Index Medicus,* the nonpareil source to worldwide medical literature.

NOTES

1. Williams, Bernard. *Miniaturised Communications* (London: The Library Association, 1970), p. 190.

2. Clearinghouse for *Federal Scientific and Technical Information* (Washington, D.C.: U.S. Department of Commerce, n.d.), p. 16.

3. Miller, Lionel. "Micrographic Applications in the Federal Government," *Journal of Micrographics* 8 (September 1974): 3–8.

4. *Microforms: A Growth Industry* (Washington, D.C.: U.S. Department of Commerce, 1969), p. 18.

5. *Educational Research Information Center (ERIC) Advance Information* (Washington, D.C.: U.S. Department of Health, Education, and Welfare, 1966), p. 4.

6. *National Archives Microfilm Publications* (Washington, D.C.: National Archives and Records Service, 1974), p. 184.

7. La Hood, Charles G. Jr., "Microfilm for the Library of Congress," *College and Research Libraries* 34 (July 1973): 291–94.

8. *Annual Report of the Librarian of Congress* (Washington, D.C.: Library of Congress, 1976) p. 89.

9. Beim, Alexander. "Micrographics Management for the Federal Government," *Journal of Micrographics* 9 (September/October 1975): 23–28.

10. Tseng, Henry P. *Complete Guide to Legal Materials in Microform* (Arlington, Va.: University Publications of America, 1976) p. 800.

Chapter 7

Library Acquisition of Microforms and Reading Equipment

ACQUISITION OF MICROFORMS

A twenty percent annual growth rate in the micrographics industry acts as a powerful magnet to attract new recruits to the ranks of more than four hundred current micropublishers, many of them offering identical source material but of varying format, reduction ratio, film stock, polarity, and indexing—enough to bedevil the already overburdened acquisitions librarian. In his *Evaluation of Micropublications,* Alan Veaner gives practical advice to anyone purchasing microforms for libraries.[1]

1. Closely examine announcements for microform projects, to establish whether material will be issued piecemeal as completed, and in what sequence—random, chronological, etc.
2. Is the publisher offering material that is available for immediate delivery, or merely a prospectus for publication at a later date?
3. Is there a firm publishing schedule with a definite termination date?
4. Does the project duplicate an already existing publication? If so, what claims does the publisher make for superiority of his product?
5. Will the publisher submit all or parts of the publication for preliminary evaluation prior to purchase?
6. Will the publisher provide replacements for any parts of the project that are technically or otherwise deficient?

7. Are selective parts of projects available if customers cannot afford the entire collection?
8. May subscribers cancel before a project has been completed? What are the terms, penalties?
9. Does the publisher do his own camera work? Does he identify types of equipment used?
10. Does the publisher certify that his product is produced on safety film stock, under appropriate standards?
11. Does the publisher's prospectus cite the reduction ratio and format?
12. Does the publisher inform libraries about various microform readers that are suitable to view his material?
13. Are indexes and catalog cards provided? Are they single cards or full sets? Which cataloging system is used?

Not all of the above criteria need to be applied for each purchase, but librarians should attempt to ascertain the reliability and past performance of micropublishers, particularly when contemplating the purchase of large and expensive sets. Colleagues in other libraries often can provide appraisals of micropublishers and individual projects. Reviews in *Microform Review* and other library journals should be examined carefully.

Proper investigation of micropublishing projects does not end when the order form is completed. Veaner recommends that a thorough physical inspection of packaging be undertaken, since improper packages can result in damage to products in shipment caused by dust, cellulose particles, or harmful chemicals. Individual units should be properly labelled and numbered, and if roll microfilm it should not be wound overly full on the reel. Roll film always should be supplied on reels, not spools, and the rolls require either paper wraparounds or sulphur-free rubber bands. Full inspection should include the use of a light box to identify any gross imperfections or mistakes in production. The last step in examination is to make a viewer inspection to compare prospectuses and finished products for such details as completeness, focus, and resolution. This physical examination of the microform purchase is best accomplished when sales agreements permit the buyer to inspect each shipment and to obtain replcements or to cancel the order if dissatisfied with any aspect of the purchase.

How do libraries remain informed about the activities of micropublishers? To obtain broad bibliographical coverage of available micropublications requires access to several guides, union lists, and current reviewing media. One of the earliest and most comprehensive tools is the *Guide to Microforms in Print* and its companion *Subject Guide to Microforms in Print.* The former is an annual cumulative guide, in alphabetical order by title, to books, journals, and other materials available from commercial micropublishers and not from the many nonprofit institutions like library centers, which also produce considerable material in microform. The *Guides,* available since 1961, list single titles and large collections, but not individual titles within collections unless those titles are offered for sale separately. Price, publisher, and type of microformat are given with each entry.

In 1965, the Library of Congress began publication of the *National Register of Microform Masters* as a means of recording complete listings of microform master copies from which duplications can be made by libraries, which may thus be spared the expense of creating unnecessary additional masters. The *Register* includes listings for pamphlets, serials, foreign PhD dissertations, and books, but not newspapers, technical reports or American PhD dissertations. Libraries are encouraged to report any holdings of master copies to the *Register* so that copies may be obtained at reasonable cost by anyone seeking access. For material unreported by the *Register,* it is necessary to consult *Newspapers on Microfilm,* published by the Library of Congress; *Government Reports Announcements and Index,* prepared by the National Technical Information Service (NTIS); and *Dissertation Abstracts* by XEROX University Microfilms, Inc. *Newspapers on Microfilm,* first published in 1948, and its successors *Newspapers in Microform: United States, 1948–72.* and *Newspapers in Microform: Foreign, 1948–72,* list thousands of newspaper titles held in the United States and abroad. The National Technical Information Service distributes reports of many government agencies which are described in detail in chapter six. *Dissertation Abstracts,* available from University Microfilms since 1938, cites vast numbers of foreign and domestic dissertations that may be procured on microfilm.

For records of filmed manuscripts, no source equals the Library of Congress's *Manuscripts on Microfilm: A Checklist of the Holdings of the Manuscript Division.* The *Checklist* cites hundreds of microfilm manuscript collections owned by many different institutions.

Microform publications of non-U.S. micropublishers are now listed in *International Microforms in Print,* by Microform Review Inc. This guide lists, by author and title, the works of some three dozen foreign micropublishers. Microform Review Inc. also offers the *Micropublishers Trade List Annual,* a collection of micropublishers' catalogs (on microfiche) with a printed index, and the *Microform Market Place, an International Directory of Micropublishing* detailing the personnel and products of the micrographics industry.

The International Microfilm Source Book, by Microfilm Publishing, Inc., also analyzes the addresses, personnel, and products of companies specializing in micrographics. And to complete the coverage, XEROX University Microfilms prepares an *International File of Microfilm Publications and Equipment,* issued on more than one hundred microfiche.

A typical but very valuable type of compilation was prepared by UPDATA Publications, 1508 Harvard St., Santa Monica, Ca., in 1973. UPDATA's *Microform Volume I,* and *Microform Reference Volume II,* prepared by Herbert Sclar, list thousands of microform titles available from domestic and foreign micropublishers through UPDATA. Serving as a jobber, UPDATA is able to procure disparate material and equipment for institutional customers and is the only large-scale jobber in micrographics presently known by the authors.

To obtain critical evaluations of new microform offerings librarians should regularly consult *Microform Review,* which publishes excellent lengthy reviews of micropublications. Reviewers stress not only the standard concerns of film type, reduction ratio, and polarity, but also whether indexing and cataloging are available, what the replacement policy for lost items is, and what options on payment are available.

Microform Review is the reviewing medium par excellence for microforms. Other library periodicals occasionally mention new micropublications or publish articles about microforms and can be accessed through *Library Literature. Library Resources and*

Technical Services has a useful annual summary of developments in micrographics, as do various volumes of the *Annual Review of Information Science and Technology*. *American Libraries, College and Research Libraries, Drexel Library Quarterly, Journal of Documentation, Library Journal, Library of Congress Information Bulletin, Library Quarterly, Library Trends, Publishers Weekly, Special Libraries,* etc., often have general articles and news notes of interest. For more specialized industrial and technical coverage, there are: *Advanced Technology—Libraries, COM Newsletter, Consumer and Library Microforms, Information—News and Sources, International Micrographics Congress Journal, Journal of Library Automation, Journal of Micrographics, Journal of Microphotography, Le Courrier de la Microcopie, Microdoc, Microfilm Newsletter, Microfilm Techniques, Microforum, Micrographics Newsletter, Micrographics Today, Microinfo, Microlist, Micropublishing of Current Periodicals, Panorama,* and *Program*. In addition, a number of office and management journals carry extensive information about micrographics in business and industry that can be of value to librarians. Some examples are: *Administrative Management, Computer World, Datamation, Government Product News, Information and Records Management, Infosystems, Modern Office Procedures, Office, Office Product News,* and *Records Management Quarterly.*

Except for *Microform Review* and indifferent attempts by several other library periodicals, none of the above publications provides in-depth coverage of new resource material published in microform. With few exceptions, the bulk of library marketing by micropublishers occurs through direct mail advertising rather than through customer representatives or journal advertising. Thus, microform and acquisition librarians acquire information on new products from a ticker tape deluge of brochures in each day's business mail.

A sample of micropublishers by subject specialty follows. Many firms issue several different types of material; however, no firm is listed in more than one category. When any micropublisher issues substantial amounts of material in two or more categories, it will be listed in the category of primary emphasis. Many companies offer microform versions of regional newspapers, periodicals, historical ephemera, etc., and every attempt has been made to cite these firms, no matter how small.

MONOGRAPHS

Academic Press, Inc.
111 Fifth Avenue
New York, New York 10003

American Microdata, Inc.
2010 Curtis Street
Denver, Colorado 80205

Australian Micropublishing Co.
67 Christie Street
St. Leonards, Sydney NSW
Australia 2065

General Microfilm Company
100 Inman Street
Cambridge, Massachusetts 02139

Irish University Press
485 Madison Avenue
New York, New York 10022

Library Microfilms
737 Loma Verde Avenue
Palo Alto, California 94303

Library Resources, Inc.
425 N. Michigan Avenue
Chicago, Illinois 60611

Lost Cause Press
750–56 Starks Bldg.
Louisville, Kentucky 40202

McClean-Hunter, Inc.
481 University Avenue
Toronto 2, Ontario, Canada

Mansell Information
3 Bloomsbury Place
London, WC1A 2QA England

Microcard Editions
5500 S. Valentia Way
Englewood, Colorado 80110

Microfiche Systems Corporation
305 E. 46th Street
New York, New York 10017

Microfilm Center, Inc.
P.O. Box 45436
Dallas, Texas 75235

Microtext Library Services
1700 State Hwy 3
Clifton, New Jersey 07013

New University Press
P.O. Box 1534
Evanston, Illinois 60204

Orion Books
58 1 chome Kanda
Jimbocho, Chiyoda-ken
Tokyo, Japan

Scholars' Facsimilies and Reprints
P.O. Box 344
Delmar, New York 12054

Somerset House
417 Maitland Avenue
Teaneck, New Jersey 07666

Southern Illinois University Press
Box 3697
Carbondale, Illinois 62901

State University of New York
99 Washington Avenue
Albany, New York 12210

University of Chicago Press
5801 S. Ellis Avenue
Chicago, Illinois 60637

University of Toronto Press
Toronto 181
Ontario, Canada

University of Washington Press
1416 N.E. 41st Street
Seattle, Washington 98195

Yushodo Film Publications
29 Saneicho, Shinjuku-ku
Tokyo, Japan

SERIALS

AMS Press, Inc.
56 East 13 Street
New York, New York 10003

American Chemical Society
1155 16th Street N.W.
Washington, D.C. 20036

American Institute of Physics
335 E. 45th Street
New York, New York 10017

Bell and Howell, Inc.
Old Mansfield Road
Wooster, Ohio 44691

Center for Research Libraries
5721 S. Cottage Grove
Chicago, Illinois 60637

Clearwater Publishing Company
792 Columbus Avenue
New York, New York 10025

Gordon and Breach, Inc.
One Park Avenue
New York, New York 10016

Information Handling Services, Inc.
P.O. Box 1154
Englewood, Colorado 80110

Institute of Electrical and Electronics
   Engineers
345 E. 47th Street
New York, New York 10017

Inter Documentation Company AG
Poststrasse 14
Zug, Switzerland

Johnson Associates, Inc.
P.O. Box 1678
Greenwich, Connecticut 06830

J.S. Canner and Company
49–65 Lansdowne Street
Boston, Massacusetts 02215

Kraus-Thompson, Inc.
KTO Microform Division
Rt 100
Millwood, New York 10546

Library Microfilms
737 Loma Verde Avenue
Palo Alto, California 94303

Library of Congress Photoduplication
   Services
10 First Street S.E.
Washington, D.C. 20540

McLaren Micropublishing
P.O. Box 972 Station F
Canada M4Y 2N9

Microfiche Publications
440 Park Avenue South
New York, New York 10016

Microfilming Corporation of America
21 Harristown Road
Glen Rock, New Jersey 07452

Microforms International Marketing
   Corporation
380 Saw Mill River Road
Elmsford, New York 10523

Micromedia, Ltd.
4 Station Approach
Kidlington, Oxford
OX5 1 JD England

Microrecords Company
3001 Vineyard Lane
Baltimore, Maryland 21218

Microtechnology, Inc.
1030 5th Avenue S.E.
Cedar Rapids, Iowa 52403

Microtek/Microfilm Techniques
820 Hanley Industrial Court
St. Louis, Missouri 63144

Minnesota Historical Society
690 Cedar Street
St. Paul, Minnesota 55101

Minnesota Scholarly Press
P.O. Box 224
Mankato, Minnesota 56001

Ohio Historical Society
1982 Velma Avenue
Columbus, Ohio 43211

Omniwest Corporation
3322 3rd East Street
Salt Lake City, Utah 48115

Oxford Microform Publications
Wheatsheaf Yard, Blue Boar Street
Oxford, England OX1 4EY

Princeton Microfilm Corporation
Alexander Road
Princeton, New Jersey 08540

State Historical Society of Wisconsin
816 State Street
Madison, Wisconsin 53706

Taylor and Francis, Ltd.
10–14 Macklin Street
London WC2B 5NF England

University Microfilms International
300 North Zeeb Road
Ann Arbor, Michigan 48106

Williams and Wilkins Company
428 E. Preston Street
Baltimore, Maryland 21202

Wm. Dawson and Sons, Ltd.
Cannon House
Folkestone, Kent CT 19 5EE England

Women's History Research Center
2325 Oak Street
Berkeley, California 94708

GOVERNMENT PUBLICATIONS

Andronicus Publishing Company
666 5th Avenue
New York, New York 10019

Brookhaven Press
901 26th Street N.W.
Washington, D.C. 20037

Carrollton Press
1647 Wisconsin Avenue N.W.
Washington, D.C. 20007

Chadwyck-Healey, Ltd.
45 South Street
Bishop Stortford, Herts CM23 3AG
England

Congressional Information Service
Montgomery Bldg.
Washington, D.C. 20014

EP Microform, Ltd.
Bradford Road
East Ardsley, Wakefield, Yorkshire
WF3 2JN England

Greenwood Press, Inc.
51 Riverside Avenue
Westport, Connecticut 06880

Hoover Institution Press
Stanford University
Stanford, California 94305

Library Resources, Inc.
425 N. Michigan Avenue
Chicago, Illinois 60611

Micromedia Limited
Box 34 Station S
Toronto, Canada M5M 416

National Technical Information
   Service
5285 Port Royal Road
Springfield, Virginia 22151

Northern Micrographics, Inc.
P.O. Box 1087
La Crosse, Wisconsin 54601

Readex Microprint Corporation
101 Fifth Avenue
New York, New York 10003

Redgrave Information Resources
   Corporation
53 Wilton Road
Westport,Connecticut 06880

Research Publications, Inc.
12 Lunar Drive
P.O. Box 3903
New Haven, Connecticut 06525

Scholarly Resources, Inc.
1508 Pennsylvania Avenue
Wilmington, Delaware 19806

Service International De Microfilms
9 Rue Du Commandant Riviere
75008 Paris, France

UNIPUB, Inc.
P.O. Box 433
Murray Hill Station
New York, New York 10016

UPDATA Publications, Inc.
1508 Harvard Street
Santa Monica, California 90404

United Nations
Room LX 2300
New York, New York 10017

U.S. Historical Documents Institute,
   Inc.
1647 Wisconsin Avenue N.W.
Washington, D.C. 20007

LEGAL MATERIALS

Butterworth Pty., Ltd.
586 Pacific Hwy
Chatswood NSW
Australia 2067

Clearwater Publishing Company
792 Columbus Avenue
New York, New York 10025

Commerce Clearing House
4025 W. Peterson Avenue
Chicago, Illinois 60646

Meiklejohn Civil Liberties Institute
1715 Francisco Street
Berkeley, California 94703

The Michie Company
P.O. Box 57
Charlottesville, Virginia 22902

Rothman Reprints
10368 West Centennial Road
Littleton, Colorado 80123

Temple University School of Law
1715 N. Broad Street
Philadelphia, Pennsylvania 19122

West Publishing Company
50 W. Kellogg Street
St. Paul, Minnesota 55102

Trans-Media Publishing Company
75 Main Street
Dobbs Ferry, New York 10522

MUSIC

Anne Marie Schnase
P.O. Box 119
120 Brown Road
Scarsdale, New York 10582

Berandol Music, Ltd.
651 Progress Avenue
Scarborough, Ontario
Canada

Dakota Graphics
9655 W. Colfax Avenue
Denver, Colorado 80215

Microprint Publishing Company
9655 W. Colfax Avenue
Denver, Colorado 80215

Sibley Music Library
Microprint Service
44 Swan Street
Rochester, New York 14604

University Music Editions
P.O. Box 192
Fort George Station
New York, New York 10040

EQUIPMENT

The microforms librarian, unlike users in business and industry who customarily work with one type of microform and, consequently, one type of reader, is faced with acquiring micrographics equipment to store and read aperture cards, microcards, microfiche, microfilm, and the manifold reduction ratios and formats available from micropublishers.

The librarian must be concerned with securing equipment that not only is capable of presenting a good image, but also one that combines to the fullest extent possible outstanding optics with optimum convenience of use. While in business applications, where random searching and spot checking constitute normal use of reading equipment, speed of access and durability are the foremost selection criteria, librarians are concerned not so much with speed of operation as with models that combine simple operating characteristics with features of design and optics that make continuous reading the mildest form of self punishment. Controls that are easily recognized are less important to the clerk in a Sears store, who performs the same search operation over and over again on the same machine, than to the student bewildered by infrequent confrontations with many different styles of film, fiche, and card readers. The provision of easily mastered controls, good resolution, and constant frame-to-frame and full frame focus are crucial to making microforms palatable in the library.

When selecting any type of microform reader, librarians should be concerned with the following equipment characteristics:

1. Visible and easily managed controls
2. Convenient loading and unloading
3. Constant frame-to-frame and full frame focus
4. Good resolution
5. Non-glare screen
6. Image Rotation
7. Full page viewing
8. Uniform screen lighting
9. Vibration free image
10. Frame location index
11. Low operating temperatures
12. Low noise levels
13. Lamps easily changed
14. Long lamps life
15. Variable light control.

Reader/Printers

1. Ease of operation, maintenance, and reliability
2. Fast print cycle
3. Jam proof operation
4. Sharp contrasting prints
5. Convenient paper and fluid loading
6. Print curl and fade resistance
7. Long paper shelf life
8. Low copy cost

In a small library possessing only 35mm microfilm, the selection of a reader for that one application is a rather simple assignment. However, in the larger library housing 16 and 35mm roll, cartridge, and cassette microfilm, microcards, and microfiche ranging in reduction from 12× to 150× and from 4 by 6 inch to 5 by 8 inch, etc., in size, the problem of selection becomes much more substantial. The great mass of material in libraries falls in the 18–24× reduction ratio range, and a reader employing a lens in that range will blow back an image approximately the same size as the original. However, any library utilizing COM or LAC, or PCMI, or any of the other variants will find that readers capable of magnifying at 42×, or 90x, or 150x are necessary. This occurs most frequently with COM-generated material which is filmed at a 42× or 48× reduction ratio. A library may have a COM application which complements more traditional microform units, and yet the traditional 18–24× readers are unsuitable for viewing COM. The librarian faces a decision on whether to buy two different readers of varying lens magnification, or a dual lens reader, or a multiple lens to be used in one brand of reader. Screen size also is very important.

Since the typical librarian rarely has the expertise to test reader models, even if access to all equipment were possible, reference to testing and reviewing media is imperative. The oldest example of these sources is *Library Technology Reports* (LTR) published by the American Library Association.[2] Here one finds exhaustive opinions by foremost experts on film stock, microfilm cartridges and cassettes, and storage cabinets . . . and detailed reviews and ratings or microform readers and reader printers. LTR tests each model, utilizing criteria developed by the National Micrographics Association (NMA), American National Standards Institute (ANSI), and the International Standards Institute (ISO) among others, attempting to simulate, as closely as possible, actual library usage. LTR tests for "Micro-image area" (established by dividing screen size by lens magnification, yielding the maximum area of any microform that can be projected on the screen), magnification, resolving power of lens, luminence and image contrast, image distortion, image rotation (can film transport mechanism be rotated to view all formats in a right-side-up position), versatility, ease of operation, and safety. Each piece of equipment also is evaluated by a group of students to rate versatility and convenience of use. Though the evaluations yield subjective results, they often can be more important to libraries than the objective results on reader performance.

Library Technology Reports (LTR), with the synthesis of test data, model specifications, prices, and excellent illustrations, should be purchased by any library owning significant numbers of microforms, or by *any* medium or large sized library, since microforms are but a very small segment of the overall coverage *LTR* devotes to library equipment and facilities.

Another valuable source of equipment data and analyses is *Micrographics Equipment Review* published by the *Microform Review* people.[3] Edited by William Hawken, the *Review* is a quarterly publication containing lavishly illustrated reports on various models suitable for libraries. It contains interesting editorial and current development news, in addition to equipment reviews similar to those in *LTR*.

Other tools of value to librarians in selecting microform readers include Hubbard Ballou's *Guide to Micrographic Equipment*;[4] Ronald Gordon's *Microfiche Viewing Equipment Guide*;[5] *Auerbach on Microfilm Readers*, and *A Guide to Microform Readers and Reader Printers*;[6] *User Evaluations of Microfilm Readers for Archival and Manuscript Materials*[7] and *Microfilm Retrieval Equipment Guide*[8] by the National Archives and Record Service; Mark McKay's *Guide to Microforms and Microform Retrieval Equipment*;[9] and George Tate's *Microform Readers—The Librarian's Dilemma*.[10]

Among the more useful of these tools are Ballou's *Guide*, which in three volumes presents extensive photographs and specifications of microform readers and reader-printers arranged alphabetically by manufacturer; Hawken's *Evaluating Microfiche Equipment*, which guides librarians to perform tests on reader resolution, magnification, focus, and image quality when selecting new fiche equipment; and the fascinating *User Evaluations of Microfilm Readers*, which summarizes a study by the National Archives covering eight of the most common library-owned microfilm readers. Though the user evaluations provide subjective data, the reactions of participants toward microfilm readers should be read and carefully considered by any librarian seeking to add new microfilm equipment to the library.

Government purchasers of microform equipment are counselled by the General Services Administration. Its *Microform Retrieval Equipment Guide* advises that when comparing microform readers "it may be found that lower cost items will satisfy all requirements." Prices vary enormously, particularly among manual versus automatic-drive microfilm readers and reader-printers and even among microfiche readers. If a library is concerned with a single application, then a single lens, standard fiche reader of good quality should be adequate. If, however, COM-generated material is present, or if there is a need for readers which also project images onto a remote screen, or if the library has fiche and film that are circulated and portability is necessary, then choices must be made about buying multiple lens for one model, or non-compatible readers, or any combination of the above. Ultimately price is an important consideration in total system costs, but it is not always the best criterion for judging quality or usefulness of any product.

Microform readers can be purchased in a variety of forms to match use environment, user needs, and cost. There are hand-held viewers suitable for spot checks; lap readers designed for portability and personal use when circulating software and reading devices from the library; larger portable readers that fold into briefcase configurations and are compact and easily carried from one location to another; desk readers (constituting the largest class of equipment found in libraries), which are usually too large to allow for anything but fixed location, usually on a desk, table, or stand; and free standing units that are self-contained, (e.g., in carrel configurations), some designed to stand alone. (Figure 12)

Optical systems are denoted by image magnification; e.g., 24× is a lens that magnifies an image 24 times. Most readers have fixed magnification or a single lens setting. Some have a design that allows for rapid, simple changes of lens to allow for varying magnifications. Fewer still have dual lens capability, whereby turning a simple switch a mechanism changes the magnification from 24× to 48×.

Placing a microform in a reader so that it is not upside down or reversed may (and with the novice user often does) take four tries with microfiche. With microfilm, where images are oriented in several different ways on the film, optical rotation devices are necessary. Camera operators may film pages in sequence with lines of text in a horizontal position reading from edge to edge of the film ("Comic"), or with lines of text in a

Figure 12

vertical position reading from bottom to top of the film ("Cine"). Pages can also be filmed in sequence using one half the film width and reversing at the end to continue filming on the remaining half ("Duo") or the front and back of documents can be filmed side by side ("Duplex"). Readers are usually designed to utilize film having images in the "Comic" orientation and yet much material available to libraries will have been done on cameras utilizing one of the other orientations. Therefore, librarians must be certain to select microfilm readers having the capability of rotating images to all possible orientations.

The electrical systems of American-manufactured readers operate on standard current of 115 volt, 60 cycle, while 220 volt, 50 cycle current is standard in many European and South American countries. Some American models can be easily adapted for special and foreign power requirements. Portable readers are available in battery-operated models, and many can be used in automobiles or airplanes. It is desirable to have readers with high quality, specially designed lamps that will maintain standard light output during the life of the bulb rather than the ordinary projection bulbs that are standard equipment in many readers. Along with cleaning of glass flats and lens, lamp replacement is probably the most frequent maintenance chore in microform facilities. Before purchasing readers, examine the placement of bulb housings and how difficult they are to reach and service. Purchase of spare bulbs at the time a new reader is ordered will prevent much grief when the original lamp dies, as it surely will, and much earlier than one would like or expect.

Because projection lamps generate light and considerable heat, projection systems and film planes of readers must be cooled to project film from damage. Desk and free standing readers usually have motor-driven blowers for cooling. Portable units often have nothing more than convection cooling, and some models have been severely criticized for dangerous electrical and heating characteristics. The optimum policy is to test models before purchase, and—especially with smaller models—to check the operating temperature of the reader to ensure that external parts do not become dangerously hot. It also is a good policy to discreetly warn users of possible temperature problems before checking a portable reader out of the library for home or office use.

Another important consideration when comparing different readers for purchase is the ease or relative difficulty of routine maintenance. Keeping readers and reader-printers clean and free of dust is an absolute necessity. Dusty screens, mirrors and lens decrease light and illumination and adversely affect the projected image. Dust on film or film holding devices damages film and reduces readibility.

Preventative maintenance, carefully following the advice offered in manufacturers' manuals, will prolong the useful life of readers and reader printers. Glass or plastic optical flats should be easily removed for cleaning and, with reader-printers, paper and chemical loading and cleaning of the printing mechanism should be possible with a minimum of difficulty.

Warranty and maintenance service varies widely among equipment manufacturers, with most warranting defective parts up to one year (normally excluding lamps). Some provide free service labor during the warranty period; others have service contracts after the warranty expires. Librarians need to examine service contracts very carefully based on the type of equipment to be covered and the available resorces in-house to perform preventative maintenance and repair. Service contracts are not cheap. They may be practical in the case of an expensive late model reader-printer, but other less complicated equipment often may be serviced and repaired by library staff.

Finally, when selecting micrographics equipment it is desirable to have the reader screen present complete pages of material at or near the original size. The difficulty libraries have in achieving this objective, particularly with microfilm readers, was aptly sumarized by George Tate.[11] The earliest microfilm projects incorporated the basic moving picture frame size of ¾ × 1 inch (18 × 24.5mm), occasionally referred to as "half-frame" but more accurately "single-frame." Early microfilm reading equipment was designed for ¾ × 1 inch film by using a micro-image area about one inch square so the projected image matched the film. Later, other microfilm cameras began using film that did not require perforations. With these cameras, the full width of the film (35mm instead of 32mm) could be utilized. The length of the film image could be extended from ⅜ inch to about 1¾ inch, and the cameras were mounted with revolving heads to allow a choice of image orientation and size. Such versatility provided savings in filming costs, but ease of use sometimes suffered as the size of images and their placement on film was left to camera operators. Typically, models of microfilm reading equipment (e.g., the ubiquitous Kodak MPE-1 Recordak reader) were produced with a film aperture of 26.5mm by 25.5mm, while Recordak microfilm cameras were producing microfilm images with 32mm widths. Users were forced to view film produced under such conditions only by moving film back and forth on the reader so as to read the entire width of the image. This experience did not improve the disposition of library users towards microforms.

Ideally, every model of microform reader should be capable of displaying a full page on the reader screen. When readers are designed to match the 32mm filming width, most camera orientations allow for full page projections. However, not all readers have this capability. In fact, the widespread adoption of 16mm microfilm for business and industrial application led many manufacturers to widen the gap between film and reader compatability. Kodak stopped production of the popular MPE-1 reader and began marketing a more costly reader which had less micro-image coverage than the MPE-1. Other manufacturers marketed readers advertised as 35mm models, when in fact they were 16mm in all respects except for film carriers capable of holding 16 and 35mm. The optics, however, were designed for 16mm film, permitting only a portion of a 35mm image to be presented on the screen. Many libraries purchased such readers, believing them to be suitable for viewing 35mm film. One wonders how much those readers contributed to the "user dislike" problem so often recounted about microforms in libraries. To illustrate how unsuitable 16mm machines are for viewing 35mm film, one need only compute the lens magnification provided as the approximate size of screen in inches needed to read a 35mm microfilm. For example, a 17× lens requires a 17 square inch screen to view a 35mm microfilm, with a one inch micro-image area (microimage area × magnification equals necessary screen size for full frame coverage), A document filmed at 17×, using the full unperforated microimage width of 1¼ inches, requires a screen 21¼ × 21¼ inches square if images are to be read without having to move the film from side to side. Very few microfilm readers have the full image capability for 35mm.

Librarians, then, should also be concerned about screen size and magnification when selecting microfilm equipment. As the use of 16mm microfilm advances in business and industry, librarians may find it even more difficult to purchase readers suitable for viewing 35mm. Unlike most business applications, library needs devolve upon many dissimilar materials. Books, periodicals, pamphlets, manuscripts—of varying sizes, color paper quality, etc.—are more easily managed on 35mm film. Librarians may never be able to successfully compete for the equipment manufacturers' attention, but we owe it to ourselves and our patrons to secure equipment that will deliver the best possible performance for the best possible price.

NOTES

1. Veaner, Allen. *Evaluations of Micropublications* (Chicago: American Library Association, 1971).
2. *Library Technology Reports* (Chicago: American Library Association, 1971).
3. *Micrographics Equipment Review* (Westport, Connecticut: Microform Review).
4. Ballou, Hubbard. *Guide to Micrographic Equipment* (Silver Spring: National Microfilm Association, 1975).
5. Gordon, R. F. *Microfiche Viewing Equipment Guide* (Alexandria, Virginia: Defense Documentation Center, 1973). (NTIS) (ERIC).
6. *Auerbach on Microfilm Readers and Reader Printers* (Philadelphia: Auerbach, 1975), 148 pages.
7. *User Evaluations of Microfilm Readers for Archival and Manuscript Materials* (Washington: Government Printing Office, 1973), 21 pages.
8. *Microform Retrieval Equipment Guide* (Washington: Government Printing Office, 1974), 88 pages.
9. McKay, Mark. *A Guide to Microforms and Microform Retrieval Equipment* (Washington: Applied Library Resources, Inc., 1972, 68 pages. (ERIC).
10. Tate, George. *Microforms—The Librarians Dilemma* (Bethesda: ERIC, 1972), 39 pages.
11. Ibid.

Chapter 8

Performance of Microforms Compared to Hard Copy, and Prospects for the Future

Research into the learning/educational value of microforms compared to books and other library material has yielded widely varying results. Published results of government, and elementary and secondary school researchers, have been generally favorable toward the positive aspects of microforms. Academic writers have been more critical in stressing the problems of bibliographic control and the less than optimum microform interface with the user. The research has ranged from testing the speed and comprehension between reading printed material in books or on microfilm, to testing the psychological effects of reading microforms.

A reading of the research will do much to dispel many of the myths about microforms, but will by no means put them all to rest.

In 1967, the Evelyn Wood Reading Dynamics organization conducted a study of students who were assigned to read a biographical novel, *I Remember, I Remember,* by Andre Maurois, and *On Liberty,* by John Stuart Mill. Fifteen students (including five better than average Reading Dynamics students) read the two books in a book edition and a microfilm edition (3 different models of film readers were used in the test) in order to test reading rate and comprehension.[1] The results of the test were:

1. Reading Dynamics students read faster on microfilm than from books with no appreciable difference in comprehension.

2. Freshmen read more slowly in biographical material on film; the juniors and seniors read faster with film. Reading *On Liberty*, freshmen read faster with film; juniors and seniors more slowly.
3. In technical biographical material there was a greater difference in comprehension between book form and microfilm. In both cases, microfilm comprehension was higher. With difficult reading material, there was no appreciable difference in comprehension among all groups tested.

Students involved in the study offered several suggestions for changes in microfilm to make it more usable for the normal and faster reader:

1. Pages should be projected singly rather than two at a time.
2. Projection should be made on a horizontal plane rather than on a vertical one.
3. Electronic potentiometer speed control should be used. Speed control should be controlled by foot, not hand.
4. Size of the projected page should be adjustable for individual readers.
5. Bright spots of projected light should be eliminated.
6. The film feed should be simple and easy to operate.
7. Projected surfaces should be sturdy enough to write on, or use as a desk.
8. Focus over the entire page should be even and sharp—this was a problem for fast readers.
9. Readers should be adjusted to normal sitting position of users.

A similar study was completed by Richard L. Coffman at the U.S. Army War College in 1972.[2] He tested graduate students to see if they could comprehend microfilmed material significantly faster than hard copy material of a similar level of difficulty. The data collection instrument was a test designed to measure each individual on both hard copy and microfilmed material. An independent variable was manipulated to ensure material of similar difficulty as measured by the Dale-Chall Readability Formula.

Results of the test were:

1. The graduate students tended to read microfilmed material slightly faster than comparable hard copy.
2. The test population tended to comprehend microfilmed material slightly faster than comparable hard copy material.
3. The difference in the reading rates and comprehension of hard copy and microfilmed material of the population sampled was not significant.

Another research project by J.M. Judisch studied the "Effect of Positive-Negative Microforms and Front-Rear Projection on Reading Speed and Comprehension."[3] Judisch noted that the majority of microfiche are produced as negative transparencies, primarily because rear projection microfiche reader designs resulted in irritating glare and hot spots, and with a negative fiche the majority of the field is dense or black thus reducing the illumination areas. Also, users generally prefer positive hard copy prints and many fiche duplicators will not produce direct positive prints from positive film. Both factors compromise the reader in Judisch's view, since the user must read a negative screen image.

To eliminate many of the objectionable qualties found in existing readers, a prototype of a new design was constructed. The new reader was designed to virtually eliminate hot spots and glare and to provide the user with a more natural viewing angle of approximately 45 degrees. The prototype was constructed to accommodate both front and rear projection systems, and screen brightness for front and rear projection was equated.

The reader-desk was equipped with two 35mm Kodak Carousel projectors, with test material taken from the Nelson-Denny Reading Test in two formats—one positive and the other negative polarity.

Two groups (professional and clerical) of sixteen subjects were tested. Each person was required to read fourteen paragraphs under different test conditions: front projection-positive, front projection-negative, rear projection-positive, and rear projection-negative. The student's assignment was to read a paragraph and answer as many of the four questions for that paragraph as possible within 90 seconds.

The results of the experiment were:

1. Both groups in the study read more rapidly under positive microfiche conditions than negative.
2. The professional group had a greater rate of comprehension under positive microfiche conditions than negative, but the comprehension rate under the two different conditions for the clerical group was nearly identical.
3. Testing of front or rear projection did not produce significant differences in reading performance between the two subject groups.

The experimenters concluded that further work was necessary to determine whether the rear projection design used in the test is superior to other rear projection readers and equal to the qualities of a front projection device. Additional research also is needed to determine if the significant differences favoring positive imagery will survive prolonged fatigue-inducing reading periods, as well as what effects familiarization with negative displays will have on the rate of reading speed and comprehension.

On the other hand, an experiment by Robert Grausnick and James Kottenstette[4] found no significant differences in user performance for positive versus negative microfiche, corroborating an earlier research result by Baldwin and Bailey.[5] (However, Baldwin and Bailey did discover significantly lower comprehension rates among students reading microfiche versus hard copy—see below.)

Grausnick and Kottenstette also found significant differences in performance between students using hard copy and microfiche in the higher and lower intelligence groups tested. No significant differences were found on any of the test exercises between hard copy and microfiche for the intermediate intelligence group. The lower intelligence group was affected most strongly by the mode of presentation; hard copy subjects in this group performed significantly better than subjects in either the positive or negative microfiche groups on four of the twelve test exercises and significantly better than the negative fiche group on a 25 minute narrative exercise. This was the only analysis which led to significant differences on any of the narrative material.

The performance of the higher intelligence group also was affected by formats, but less dramatically. In this group performance with hard copy was significantly better than performance with either positive or negative image microfiche on a figure identification test, and better than the negative-image group only on graph and symbol translation tests, which are very dependent on recognition of individual type characters or precise visual discrimination.

In the Baldwin and Bailey experiment, the researchers hypothesized that the ability of students to assimilate and utilize information contained in technical training materials is the same for each of the following methods of presentation: (1) material presented as black on white offset copy, (2) material presented via microfiche with positive image, and (3) material presented via microfiche with negative image.[6]

Twelve different tests were administered to three different groups of U.S. Air Force trainees. One group received the material on offset copy (hard copy), the second group received the identical material on positive image microfiche, and the third group received the test material on negative image microfiche.

Statistical analysis of the data revealed that in three of the twelve tests the mean score for trainees receiving offset copy was significantly greater than the mean score for those using either positive or negative microfiche. For the remaining nine tests there were no significant differences among the three groups. In none of the twelve tests were mean scores for positive image microfiche significantly different from mean scores for negative image fiche.

In another experiment by Grausnick and Kottenstette no significant differences in performance between hard copy and microform were observed.[7]

The researcher converted a thirty hour instructional sequence on basic computer operation into negative and positive microform formats. Students in three experimental classes used the microform presentation both in the classroom and in their

residences. The microform use patterns and course perform-
ances of these students were determined and compared with
use patterns and the performance of students in three control
classes in which identical instructional materials in hard copy
were employed. The major result of the comparative analysis
was that trainees used the microform material effectively and
intensively over a one week period. No significant performance
decrements were observed in the experimental classes.

Among academic libraries, far fewer experiments testing
microform usage and comparisons between hard copy and microform material have been reported than with the work of
government researchers.

However, several conferences have been held concerning microform applications, and a number of innovative programs
utilizing microforms in lieu of paper copy have been reported
in the literature.

In December 1970 a conference titled, "Microform Utilization: The Academic Library Environment" was held at the
University of Denver.[8] Chaired by James P. Kottenstette, the
conference brought together a distinguished group of academic
librarians to "develop information and to probe the difficulties
of managing and using library microforms." The focus of the
conference was to treat the library administrator as a mediator
between competing interests. First, he must deal with technolo-
gists who generate new solutions to problems of acquisition and
storage where microforms are very important. The administrator also interacts with micropublishers who have their own ideas
of the need for new microform projects in the library. And, the
administrator comes into contact with the user of microforms.
Somehow the library administrator must "integrate and balance
this combination of forces and interests."

The conclusions of conference participants, both industry
representatives and library administrators, appear below:

I. Recommendations concerning bibliographic control of microforms:

Support and encourage the Association of Research Libraries'
study of bibliographic controls conducted by Felix Reichmann.

Establish a formal position concerning those bibliographic tools
that the publisher should be expected to provide with his publications.

Support this expectation through boycott if necessary. The library community has the necessary professional associations to both define expectations and to identify acceptable publications and the library community should accept this responsibility.

Encourage support of the National Register of Microform Masters. The Register is presently incomplete because libraries have not reported to it, and many are ignorant of it.

Request the Library of Congress to expand the capability of the National Register and consider the creation of microform analytics in more complete form.

II. Recommendations concerning microform viewers:

Work to better identify the types of reader equipment that are suited to the varied uses of an educational environment, and encourage the U.S. Office of Education to continue its sponsorship of research in this area.

Endorse the integrated reference carrel concept, which equipment is designed for reference work as opposed to research or study uses. The reader-carrel should be designed to facilitate relatively short duration microform transactions where the user clearly understands his immediate needs; and includes reader, work surface, and control of local environment including illumination; this equipment to facilitate a major portion of current library microform reader requirements. Equipment manufacturers should be alerted to this equipment need.

III. General Recommendations:

Work to create training programs to produce qualified people for careers in photoduplicaton; the paraprofessional concept should be developed in concert with the microform industry.

Suggest the inclusion of microform technology in the curricula of library schools so that graduating librarians will be versed in microform use; and encourage the training of currently active librarians in the use of microforms through seminars and short courses developed specifically for their benefit.

Create at some institution a library of microform technology which is complete, recognizing the critical need for centralized information relating to all facets of microform technology operations.

Consider the premise that a total microform system is the key issue; development of a total approach to library microform handling and use will answer many separate problems such as bibliographic controls, indexing, use modes, equipment design

> and quality and that total system design is the long-term approach to achieving useful interface between microforms and information transfer in libraries.

> Understand that the library community has played a passive role in the evolution of library-related microforms and that it must begin to define its own needs so that the industry can respond to requirements rather than attempting to define them.

Several libraries have reported on specific applications where microforms have been substituted for book copy in instructional programs. One such program with wide-ranging implications for future expansion in institutions of higher learning was the conversion of class reading lists to microfiche at San Jose State University.[9] At the Department of Librarianship, San Jose State, concern was expressed over the large number of expensive required readings assigned to a student body which was largely commuting to classes and either employed or concerned with raising a family. An expensive textbook provided the basic learning tool for the class, along with the instructor's assigned readings that were kept on reserve for short-term reference. Familiarity with lower costs of microfiche led to an experiment utilizing required readings in microform rather than hard copy. Some unanswered questions concerned the amount of student resistance to be encountered with microforms, the costs and technical problems of obtaining and microfilming readings, and the differences if any that would occur with completion of assignments and leaning.

The Readings List selected for the experiment was taken from a Foundations of Librarianship, multi-section class with a relatively stable syllabus and taught regularly by the same two teachers. The syllabus was revised so that all the readings included were required and all recommended readings that could not be obtained locally in multiple copies were eliminated. Three sections of the course were used in the experiment. One section used microfiche copies of the readings—this was the class section composed of part-time and commuter students who had the greatest difficulty in gaining access to required readings.

Copyright release permission for microfilming readings was

requested by letter from several publishers, only one of whom insisted on payment of a small royalty.

At the end of the semester a survey questionnaire was distributed to the class to be returned anonymously. All students in the test section used the microfiche readings at least ten times; seventy-five percent of the students used the microfiche over twenty times. Students were able to check out some portable readers for use at home; others sought out fiche readers in other libraries near home. No student reported use of a reader printer to obtain page copy. About seventy-five percent of the students reported they had thoroughly read sixty percent or more of the assigned readings. No significant difference was noticed between the test section and other sections using paper copies in this regard.

Two-thirds of the test class rated the use of microreadings as "better" than the printed materials. Only one student rated the system "much less" convenient, and this was primarily because not enough portable readers were available. Nine students felt microforms made completion of reading assignments easier, six perceived no difference, and three felt it was more difficult.

The characteristic cited as high in aggravation by two-thirds of the class was viewing fatigue. Only five students reported they read more articles in microform than they would have read using only print resources during the test.

When asked if they would purchase microfiche readings in the bookstore at $4.00 per set instead of having to rely on reserve room readings, thirteen students said they would "definitely" or "probably" purchase a set of fiche, four students said "possibly," and only one replied "probably not." As to whether students would be willing to purchase personal portable microfiche readers (about $100)—a factor that would greatly enhance success of this and similar programs—reaction was decidedly negative even though this was a class of librarians who probably were more familiar with use of the equipment than the average student.

More favorable results were obtained with assigned readings on microfiche when sufficient portable readers were purchased by the library for students at the University of South Africa.[10] The University emphasized correspondence courses, and the process of sending books out to students by mail was costly and time-consuming. A pilot project in 1971 enrolled twenty-seven students in a library science course where assigned readings would be in fiche, not paper. The objectives were to discover the reaction of students, the willingness of publishers to cooperate on copyright, and the possibility of obtaining suitable, low cost readers.

The initial project was very successful, and the University decided to purchase an additional 300 readers in order to extend the project to include all library science students. A total of 333 students were supplied with fiche readers and lists of the books available on fiche. In all, 266 books were used in the course, of which seventy-three percent were approved for filming by the publishers.

Students responding to a questionnaire about the program confirmed the success of the earlier experiment. Microfiche was regarded as completely acceptable by thirty-five percent of the students, thirty-eight percent regarded it as acceptable, and fourteen percent as reasonably acceptable. Only fourteen percent of the students had serious doubts about the efficacy of fiche, apart from eight percent who did not reply to the question. The most unfavorable reaction regarded reading speed and eye strain. Forty-seven percent of the students thought they read more slowly with fiche, against thirty-two percent who maintained the same speed, and nine percent who read faster.

The overall chief advantages to the students who used fiche readings were their guaranteed availability for use and the extended loan periods available to commuter and correspondence students.

At the Bell Telephone Laboratories, the Library conducted a study in 1971 to evaluate microfiche as a possible alternative to paper copy for distributing technical information.[11] Using fiche instead of paper offered large potential savings in publication, distribution, and storage of technical report literature at Bell, in addition to faster response time and greater accessibility to information.

About 250 people in one laboratory division were selected for the study with the understanding that participation was wholly voluntary. Reading equipment was purchased and placed in convenient locations throughout the division. Some readers were portable. The test with fiche was scheduled to run for six months so that "participants would have ample time to accustom themselves to reading fiche reports and settle down to a regular pattern of use."

During the test, requests for fiche copies of reports were serviced within twenty-four hours of receipt by forwarding a diazo duplicate to the requester for permanent retention. Full sized prints from fiche were made on demand and also sent within twenty-four hours to requesters. If a requester then asked for a full paper copy, it was done after circulation of the report was completed to all Bell staff.

After the test had run for six months a questionnaire was sent to everyone participating in the study. The questionnaire was purely subjective and measured attitudes toward microfiche. The two most frequent criticisms expressed in the questionnaire concerned inconvenience caused by insufficient numbers of fiche readers and poor quality of readers and fiche. Asked if they would agree to continue receiving fiche, fifty-five percent of the participants answered yes. Only five percent of the respondents expressed dissatisfaction with overall service of the Technical Reports Center during the test.

During the test period, users requested hard copy (blowback and complete reports) for only twelve percent of the microfiche reports they received. In response to the question, "Are you keeping the microfiche copy?" sixty-two percent of the users gave an affirmative answer, so it was assumed by the experimenters that "microfiche was an acceptable substitute for hard copy documents in personal collections" at Bell Telephone Laboratories.

In another study by the Director of the Library at Research Laboratories in the Environmental Science Services Administration, Ralph Lewis examined the effects on users of the large scale conversion to microfiche taking place throughout government.[12]

Questionnaires were sent to engineers and technicians who were now receiving reports in fiche rather than paper. The answers reflected the users' attitude toward the suitability of fiche as a medium for the dissemination of technical information: The response showed an "overwhelming lack of enthusiasm." Positive opinions were outnumbered by almost two to one. Furthermore, many of those who considered microfiche to be acceptable added significant comments that modified their acceptance. For example, many indicated that microfiche would be acceptable for materials that were to be scanned for relevance, but that material needed for study or use in research were needed "in hard copy if they were needed at all." Some acknowledged that microfiche might afford some savings in space and distribution costs, but that the user was not being considered.

The author of the study concluded that "the complaints registered in these comments are the same complaints librarians have always heard about materials in microform. The preferences indicated are no different than preferences of other scholars. The problems that have plagued the use of microforms are still very real."

CONCLUSIONS

Thus, the substitution of microforms for hard copy among users in government and academia has produced mixed reactions. In 1962, one writer predicted that "we are in the early stages of the microbook revolution . . . with business records, library copies of back issues of newspapers, thousands of PhD dissertations, and many tens of thousands of unpublished and mimeographed research reports for government agencies, stored on film."[13]

The overriding cause of conversion from paper to film has been economic, yet as we have seen, microform "may be cheaper but it is definitely not easier on the user." In study after study, the dissatisfactions of users have been chronicled, suggestions have been tendered on improving readers, but the interface between man and machine remains an enigma.

Perhaps, as Les Burchinal contends, the greatest potential growth of microform use will not occur in higher education, or even among government agencies, but instead in "the hands of elementary and secondary school students."[14] The much larger size of the elementary-secondary school population compared to that of post-secondary schools, and the mutimedia approach —along with experiments with more independent study and use of technology to support learning—augur well for acceptance of microforms at the lower school levels.

A surprisingly large number of instructional packages are available to schools. For example, the XEDIA Program from Xerox attempts to establish a link between the microform reader screen and television with a selection of 2000 high interest books on microfiche geared to the K–9 audience. Book selections cover a broad range of reading and interest levels. Some are curriculum oriented, exploring facets of language arts, social sciences, and science. Others emphasize reading skills and are especially useful for remedial reading and special education classes where students may need a number of high-interest, easy-to-read books.

Another more specialized program aimed at secondary schools is the "New York Times School Microfilm Collection," a selection of newspaper reels designed to enrich the teaching of Social Studies and American History.

As more students are introduced to these and similar learning materials in microform, Burchinal argues that microform usage will move from the innovative stage, where it now stands, to a condition of acceptance and widespread adoption where a majority of users will look favorably toward microforms as a means of providing low-cost materials.

Costs, unquestionably, are the key to understanding the microform revolution in libraries. Who would choose to read a PhD dissertation or a technical report in microform rather than paper if the costs of the two formats were the same? Microforms are less familiar and less convenient to use in all but the rarest circumstances, but they cost less! And for libraries everywhere, the materials budget is like a tuna fisherman's net that as the years go by brings in fewer and fewer fish.

Microforms make it possible for libraries to collect technical reports, newspapers, periodicals, and a great many other materials that would otherwise be unobtainable with the funds available, and this applies not only to academic libraries where the situation seems to be worst, but also to school, special, and government libraries as well.

The task for librarians is to work for the gradual improvement of conditions under which microforms are used. Primarily, this improvement should address library facilities for microforms, including a better environment and professional staffing, but it should also address the need for equipment manufacturers to continue to develop improved readers, especially portable models. Less can be expected, however, from new technology than from the efforts librarians are capable of making to enhance microforms usage.

Reichmann and Thorpe discovered that the overwhelming majority of 190 libraries responding to their survey on bibliographic control were not satisfied with present circumstances and in fact deplored the "lack of adequate control" of microforms.[15] What hope is there of creating a favorable attitude toward microforms when the initial contact by the user at the card catalog falls short of providing comprehensive information on available microforms and their location in the library. Descriptive cataloging of microforms should be no less satisfactory than cataloging of books and periodicals. Micropublishers should be encouraged to always prepare cataloging for sale with microform collections, but when cataloging is not available with purchases, libraries must assign adequate resources for processing microforms and for creating access points wherever possible. Only then will the synthesis of adequate bibliographic access and competent professional assistance begin to overcome the pejorative aspects of microforms, so that libraries at last can take advantage of the full promise of the Microform Revolution.

NOTES

1. Wood, Evelyn. "Microfilm Reading Rate and Comprehension Study," (Westport: Reading Dynamics, 1967). (NTIS Report AD770 536)

2. Coffman, Richard L. "An Inquiry into the Effect of Microfilm on the Graduate User's Reading Rate and Comprehension." (Carlisle Barracks, Pa.: Army War College, 1972). (NTIS Report AD-760 916)

3. Judisch, J.M. "The Effect of Positive-Negative Microforms and Front-Rear Projection on Reading Speed and Comprehension," (State College, Pa.: HRB-Singer, Inc, 1969). (NTIS AD 692551)

4. Grausnick, Robert R. and Kottenstette, James P. "A Performance Evaluation: Microfiche versus Hardcopy," (Denver: University of Denver, 1971). (NTIS AD 734 740)

5. Baldwin, T.S. and Bailey, L.J. "Readability of Technical Training Materials Presented on Microfiche vs Offset Copy," *Journal of Applied Psychology,* February 1971, pp. 37–41.

6. Ibid.

7. Grausnick, Robert R. et al. "Microform Use in a Technical Training Environment—An Experiment," (Denver: University of Denver, 1971). (NTIS-AD 733 686)

8. Morrison, Alta Bradley, ed., *Microform Utilization: The Academic Library Environment* (Denver: University of Denver, 1970), p. 231.

9. Butler, Brett B. and West, Martha W. "Microreadings: Easing Obstacles to Library Distribution of Information," *The Journal of Micrographics* 7 (July–August 1974): 17–22.

10. Willemse, John. "Microfiche as a Means of Providing Students with Literature," *Microform Review* 3 (January 1974): 26–29.

11. Christ, C.W. Jr., "Microfiche: A Study of User Attitudes and Leading Habits," *Journal of the American Society for Information Science* 23 (January–February 1972) 30–35.

12. Lewis, Ralph W. "User's Reaction to Microfiche: A Preliminary Study," *College and Research Libraries* 4 (July 1970): 260–268.

13. Platt, John. "Where Will the Books Go?" *Horizon* 5 (September 1962): 42–47.

14. Burchinal, Lee G. "Uses of Microfilm in Educational Institutions," *The Journal of Micrographics* 7 (January 1974): 107–112.

15. Reichmann, Felix and Thorpe, Josephine. *Bibliogaphic Control of Microforms* (Westport: Greenwood Press, 1972).

Chapter 9

Setting Up a Microform Facility

Although micropublishing began seriously in 1938, the availability and the acquisition of large collections of materials in microforms did not increase greatly until the early 1970s. Perhaps the uncertainty and slowness of production and distribution in the early days contributed to libraries' not taking the new form seriously enough to make adequate plans for its use. Some new buildings designed in the middle and late 60s provided only minimal space and buildings of the 70s may have provided space for a microform center, but not sufficient electrical outlets in all the areas desirable for displaying the newer Computer Output Microfilm (COM) services.

The revolution in microforms continues. Ignoring microforms did not make them disappear and casual treatment has compounded the difficulties in overcoming resistance to their use. The momentous change in the microform situation requires that a new look at the forms be taken. They should be viewed not merely as substitutes for paper copies, but judged for their own characteristics. They are lightweight, compact, portable, have great storage capacity, and can preserve and disseminate copies of rare or fragile originals. Variable image size, cheapness and ease of duplication, availability of hard copies as needed, and ease of replacement are further merits pointed out by Allen Veaner who urges libraries to "capitalize on the unique capabilities of a new method of storing, retrieving, and using information."[1]

Collections of microforms in libraries have increased dramatically over the past eight years as revealed by comparing ARL (Association for Research Libraries) statistics for those

years. The larger university libraries in the United States holding a total of 34.4 million units of microform in 1969/70[2] held
106.3 million units in 1977/78,[3] the median increasing from
412.8 thousand units to 1.1 million. Boston University, with the
lowest count in 1969/70 of 98.5 thousand, reports 944.4 thousand in 1977/78.

Libraries with large holdings have added relatively few items
during the period, while libraries with smaller holdings have
grown in response to several factors. The availability in microform of materials not otherwise affordable by the library, because of their expense or their fragile original forms, presents
an attractive consideration. The high cost and dwindling amount
of space available for housing hard copy materials in decreasing
demand or in deteriorating or mutilated condition provides
further impetus for expanding the microform collection. Binding costs of periodicals and the increased frequency of items
which are published only in microform or are collected in microform sets for easier use have had their influence on the
collecting habits of smaller libraries. Newspapers on film continue to be the most obvious source of collector and user satisfaction.

In making plans for setting up a microform facility, consideration must be given to all the characteristics of microforms and
the ways in which they may be stored, serviced, and used to the
best advantage. The same, if not more, care and concern must
be exhibited for the microform area(s) that have been shown in
establishing the other well-run service areas of the library.
Where staff- and user-resistance has surfaced sufficiently to
threaten the success of the facility, additional efforts will be
needed to bring about a change of attitude in both groups.
When the librarians are persuaded to adopt a positive approach
to the content of the collection and the merits of the reading
machines and copiers, the first important step will have been
taken to encourage users.

The question of user satisfaction/user resistance continues to
plague the collectors and servicers of micromaterials. But as
collections expand geometrically, more library users in pursuit
of information will find it essential to become familiar with the
forms, the shelving, the readers, and the printers that produce
hard copy or microfiche duplicates. Users of all ages and per-

suasions may avoid the microform trauma as long as possible and be led only unwillingly to its presumed treasures. They may have to be coaxed into accepting the inevitable, while others, even now, report to a microform center first to see if their needs can be met there before they tackle hard copy.

The factors that subvert user satisfaction must be examined and attended to in some fashion by planning the microform facility and introducing it to the library community. The first objection to the reduced format on microfilm, microfiche, or microcard, is that it neither looks nor feels like a book, magazine, or typewritten report. The form of a page shows better, to the naked eye, on the fiche or card than on the film—until the film is unwound—but it is still vague. The microform, even if placed properly into the viewer with the light turned on and the focus knobs adjusted to show the page, may then expose white print on a black background. The user has both the intrusion of a glass screen *and* a negative image between him/her and the expected familiar page. The fact that the negative image creates less glare than a positive black on white is small comfort to the person who preferred a printed paper page in the first place. A smear or blot of foreign matter on the film or screen may obscure several words and even though the reader can tell what the words are, frustration mounts.

The user becomes conscious of the surrounding light being too much or too little, then the heating pipes begin to clunk or sizzle at uneven intervals. Chairs scrape along the floor as other users move in determinedly to begin an assignment or move out in jubilation or disgust. The whir of several automatic film advance/rewind mechanisms sets up a cacophony with the unoiled wheels of a booktruck of film boxes to be shelved making their agonizing complaint down the length of the area. Assuming the operation of Murphy's Law—that anything that can go wrong will—there are innumerable things that will go wrong in a microform operation that has been casually assembled without consideration for users, materials, and equipment.

There are studies of space use, surveys of user attitudes, equipment evaluations, and discussions on the advantages of the various microformats to aid planners of facilities in new buildings or revisers of older ones. But, as James Prevel stated in 1970 there is still "no cookbook method for what we are going to do in libraries with microforms. No rules saying how many square feet of space to use, number of readers to provide, number of microforms to stock because we are still in the very dynamic stage of development of microforms and in establishing their use."[4]

Assuming the setting up of a relatively problem-free facility, the rate of increase of its use cannot be known, but it must be projected at least in terms of reading stations. Excellent service is likely to encourage acceptance of the forms by those who have witnessed the service and tell their friends about it. Additional users will come from among those who attend orientation, instruction, or tour sessions. The number of new materials or services appearing in microformat is another unknown. College catalogs, telephone directories, and other quick-reference tools —whether found in a microform center or in the reference area—will encourage the habit of using micromedia as a normal part of information gathering. Use of Computer Output Microfilm (COM) catalogs and other tools along with on-line search services by way of a cathode ray tube (CRT) terminal should gradually break down the barrier of the machine between the user and the material. Again, an increase in converts.

A setting designed and operated to satisfy users will satisfy staff who service it as well as provide the environment most conducive to the care and preservation of the materials and equipment. Problems posed by microforms were identified by Donald Holmes in 1969 in reports of a study for the Association of Research Libraries, available in the ERIC Documents series. In the first report Holmes pointed out the reasons why they had not reached their potential.[5] With regard to the materials: their variety and the special equipment necessary for storage and use; loss or damage resulting from careless handling by acquisitions, cataloging, and users; and, the lack of an adequate system for bibliographical control and optimum retrieval. With regard to the physical environment: improper lighting, temperature, and humidity; inadequate provision and care of the equipment and furnishings; and, ineffective means of administering the microform operation. External influences noted by Holmes are: lack of a method for insuring that producers of microforms observe appropriate production standards, and lack of authoritative structures to effect a rational decision-making process in

determining the appropriate type of microform for reproducing a given type of document.

Most libraries having large collections of microforms have some kind of central facility. In addition to the central area, some materials and readers may be located in subject areas or in library departments where they are used as working tools by staff members. Smaller libraries, public and college, may elect to centralize equipment, but decentralize materials, or to decentralize both. The users' approach to microforms and the staff and space available to house them should determine a given library's program. Centralization does provide the opportunity to create the best environment in one location.

The various factors in providing a good user environment are interdependent, but materials and machines are essential to start with. Materials must be stored so that a particular fiche or reel may be easily found. Cabinets, economic with space and designed to house large numbers of fiche or roll film, may be lined up against walls or used as room dividers, depending on the layout of the area. Microcards (3 × 5 inch opaque photo-reduced positive images) may be housed in cabinets that also hold 3 × 5 inch microfiche, but not in the same tray. It is generally wise not to interfile different media because of the uncertainty of the interaction of chemicals in the composition of the medium, acidity of paper, etc. Although the use of Microprint (opaque photo-reduced positive image on sheets, usually 6 × 9 inch) has decreased in new publications, it does continue in ongoing sets such as U.S. government publications and United Nations documents. The sheets are supplied in labeled boxes that can be shelved on regular book shelves. Book shelves are also required for hard copy indexes and other reference items needed in the microform area.

In some libraries indexes remain in the Reference Department if it gives assistance in locating information in microform. This can work well if the Reference Department is adjacent to, or nearby, the microform holdings. When the areas are on separate levels or otherwise geographically apart, it is essential for the microform staff to have the indexes and guides handy to assist the users. Duplication of indexes should be kept to a minimum, but not to jeopardize the success of the service.

Microfilm, transparent photographic film, usually 16mm or

35mm in width with positive or negative images, on reels or in cartridges, may be stored in boxes or Princeton files on standard book shelves. For saving space there are metal cabinets with trays which can accommodate up to 1,000 reels of 35mm or 2,000 reels of 16mm film in easily retrievable order. Carousel-type units also are available for roll film cassettes or cartridges.

Microfiche, transparent sheets of photographic film, usually 3 × 5 inch or 4 × 6 inch with positive or negative images, may be stored in trays, accommodating either size, in metal cabinets. Ultrafiche, with a higher reduction ratio resulting in 2,000 to 3,000 pages per sheet as compared with the usual microfiche of 45 to 60 pages, may be 3 × 5 inch or 4 × 6 inch with a positive image.

Aperture cards, a microfilm image combined with a key-punched card, and with eye-readable access information, come in various sizes, but commonly 3¼ × 7⅜ inch. They may have one image or up to eight page-size images in one 35mm frame and are usually used for storing large documents, such as engineering drawings. Aperture cards are not likely to be found in great numbers in the collection except in special libraries.

The super reading machine that could handle all the variety of existing microforms has not been invented, except in fantasy. The complexities of such an imaginary piece of equipment would require magicians to operate it and keep it in repair. Instead, there are machines for each type of microform. Some variations in reduction ratio of images can be handled by changing lenses, and some machines will accomodate more than one form (e.g., fiche and 35mm roll film, with an accessory part purchased separately). Ultrafiche requires its own reader as do the micro-opaques, although the Readex micro-opaque reader accommodates microfiche but not as well as the usual microfiche readers. Maintaining a microform reader and installing any accessories should be easy. Lamp and lens changing should be simple operations and cleaning the optical and film carrier system should present no problem for the trained operator.

The Reader/Printer, or Printer used to produce paper copy from one or more of the microforms, is a more complicated machine than the Reader to care for and tend. It uses paper, coated or uncoated, in sheets or rolls and a fluid or toner in the printing process. A Reader/Printer—sometimes with, sometimes without, attachments—may produce copy from microfilm, microfiche, and aperture cards. Copy from ultrafiche requires its own printer as do the micro-opaques, but again, the micro-opaque printer can handle microfiche. *Library Technology Reports* publishes evaluations of Readers, Reader/Printers, and microfiche duplicators on an ongoing basis.[6] Detailed information is given on the construction and working of the machines, supplies needed, accessories available, and whether or not a good operator's manual is provided by the manufacturer or distributor. *Micrographics Equipment Review*[7] and the *Guide to Microproduction Equipment,* edited by Hubbard Ballou,[8] are also excellent sources for information about equipment.

There is discussion and disagreement among users and librarians about the appropriate furniture on which the machines should be placed. Some prefer microfiche readers on open tables and microfilm readers in carrels, possibly on the assumption that microfiche are used for shorter periods of time. That users of microfilm wish to settle in comfortably and privately for a long session of reading may be the result of the kind of material that has been provided on microfilm. As more back-runs of periodicals appear on microfiche this may change. In Holmes's second study he suggested a design for a reading carrel to provide for adjustment in height and reading angle of the machine to counteract the fatigue caused by the rigid line of sight normally existing between reader and machine.[9] In 1971 a pilot model was built as a prototype design with a machine platform that revolved sideways and tilted backward and forward. It was reportedly unsuccessful because it turned too stiffly and flopped instead of tilted.[10] Planners of the microform facility at New York University's new Bobst Library (1973) designed their own reading carrel with a movable platform that can be raised or lowered a maximum of 3 inches and that can be turned laterally by hand. A secretary (posture) chair also adds lateral and vertical movement for the user. The reading station, a double unit approximately five and one-half feet by four and one-half feet, includes a writing area, book shelf and small lamp. Film readers only are housed in these carrels at the Bobst.[11]

A secretary chair can, of course, be used with a stationary carrel to provide some mobility. There must be writing space at the side or the front of the machine and some machines should be placed on the right side of the carrel to provide comfortable space for left-handed users. Provisions, too, must be made for wheelchair access to the area, with sufficient aisle space and accommodation at the reading stations.

Lighting in the microform area should be of low intensity so that the screen images may be easily read, but it must be adequate for moving about and for using indexes or other tools. Fifteen to twenty foot candles at the work surface seems to be a general rule. Daylight can cause reflections on the screens and must be reduced in some way by curtains or dividers. Indirect lighting that can be dimmed by local switches may solve the problem in the machine area.

The suppression of sound in the microform area is extremely important. Carpeting is a must to cut back on the noise of moving chairs and especially to dampen the noise of automatic film advance/rewind accessories. Carpeting, too, is desirable for its dirt-trapping abilty, and its cleaning by vacuuming does not raise dust. The use of partitioned areas or carrels is an additional help, along with wall panels of sound-absorbing material. Another essential room condition is temperature and humidity control. If the building itself is not air-conditioned and humidified for the comfort of people and for the protection of all materials, special temperature and humidity controls should be provided for film, which becomes brittle with low humidity.

It is very difficult, probably impossible, to declare any one factor in the condition of the microform area, the collection, and its equipment for storage and use, as being more important than any other in making the area a successful venture for user satisfaction. Staffing the area is, however, very high on the list. Depending on the library organization and the attributes of staff members, very satisfactory operations may be managed by either a professional librarian or a library technician, but someone must be specifically in charge of the area. The most important attribute is a positive attitude about microforms along with administrative ability and mechanical aptitude. Thorough knowledge of the collection and the tools for retrieving information, intimate familiarity with the operation of all the machines, and an appreciation for the physical nature of the materials, can make any staff member an enthusiastic proponent of the microform way. The enthusiasm affects the users when the staff member is prepared to help with locating the material and demonstrating the use of the machines. Instructions for machine use printed on the machines or affixed to them do not always explain every detail and it may be the unexplained detail that gets the user into some difficulty that a demonstration can prevent.

Whatever the staff of the microform area can do to encourage a positive attitude on the part of the library staff in general, and the reader services staff in particular, will redound to the credit and credibility of the microform area. Tours and demonstrations for staff members should be as carefully planned as those for students. The contrast of the bulk and awkwardness of use of paper copy versus film copy for newspapers is a good ploy along with a quick sample retrieval of an item from conference proceedings, e.g. on fiche, as opposed to a trip to the stacks to locate the proper pages in the proper volume of hard copy. Demonstrating the wealth of material in the ERIC series may be the pièce de résistance. The person who has been searching everywhere for an item and suddenly finds it in microform in the collection can almost be guaranteed to be a happy user, but such an occurrence cannot be counted on to happen at the most propitious time for public relations. Librarians are very frequently more anti-microform than users are. They have resisted the forms that have already become part of the library's life and now the same negativism is showing up with regard to COM (Compuer Output Microform). A librarian can affect or infect a user before the user ever arrives at the Microform area. Thus it behooves the proponents of microform, the staff of the area, and any other influential positive-minded librarians to spread the word to their colleagues. Librarians will continue to be devotees of the book, but they must not be blind to other methods of displaying information. There are trade-offs which should be explored and exploited to provide the best possible information dispersal. On the chance that insecurity in using the machines has prevented the staff members from investigating the media fully and feeling comfortable in recommending their use, instruction and hands-on operation should be encouraged, even required, for those who serve people.

The microform staff should include those who can make minor repairs on the machines and do cleaning and maintenance. Depending solely on contracted service for repairs is to jeopardize the success of the operation. "Out of order" signs on several machines, although better than no warning, reinforces negative feelings and may cause indefinite backsliding for the near-convert. The supervisor of the area should be encouraged to visit other installations, to keep up with the literature, and to learn all that he or she can about micrographics.

For inspecting, cleaning, and repairing microforms there should be a work area, preferably a walled-in room. The room can house spare parts such as bulbs and optical flats (glass plates between which the fiche is placed or roll film threaded) and provide temporary storage shelving. Equipment for inspecting and splicing film must be provided and this is a good place to house a fiche duplicator if fiche copy is available for sale or for loan when the library circulates portable fiche readers.

The Bobst Microform Center, New York University, carefully developed in consideration of the requirements for user satisfaction, showed continued increase in use. Statistics of users were kept for a twelve-week period in the fall of the first three years it was open. They showed an eighty-four percent increase in 1974–1975 over 1973–1974 and another forty percent increase in 1975–1976.[12] A study of the attitudes of users was done by means of a questionnaire completed by users selected randomly. Comments were solicited along with the specific answers to questions. Of those who responded, eleven percent were faculty and visitors, eighty-nine percent graduate and undergraduate students; forty-six percent used the Center seldom or occasionally, fifty-four percent used it often or frequently (i.e., once a month at least, or once a week or more often). Two-thirds of the respondents spent one to four hours at a time; the other third spent less than one hour. The attitudes of users toward microforms for research and information gathering were heavily positive as were their opinions on room comfort, equipment, quality and condition of the microforms, assistance received, and room arrangement. The general comments, too, were favorable and complimentary, highly rewarding to the planners who had spent so much time and thought on all the possible factors involved in providing an attractive, comfortable, service- and people-oriented facility.[13] In any new experience, people are acutely aware of their own initial reactions, which are very likely to become permanent, and thus the library should provide the best it can for these first impressions.

In 1976 Francis Spreitzer conducted a study of library microform facilities for *Library Technology Reports*.[14] He found four arrangement variations for collections and reading areas: (1) Centralized reading areas with most frequently used materials, others in the stacks. (2) A connecting two-room suite with the collection in one room, readers in the other with attendants at the juncture of the two parts. (3) Decentralized facilities in libraries organized on a divisional plan, with each area equipped for microform use. (4) The integrated plan with some part of the microform collection shelved with full-size materials of the same kind, e.g. periodicals. From several dozen libraries—large, small, new, old, academic and public—he selected four as outstanding examples of their type of microform area. The aesthetic appeal of each, although different from the other, is as attractive as the rest of the library of which it is a part.

The three academic installations at Michigan State University, University of Wisconsin at Milwaukee, and the University of Denver Penrose Library are located in buildings new or remodeled in 1972–73 and are in desirable areas. Michigan State has its microforms centrally serviced, except for government documents in the documents area, but shares its third-floor area with Art and Maps. Milwaukee has a room especially for microforms, while Denver has an L-shaped area in an openplan building. Both Denver and Milwaukee use the lower level, but not a basement area. All three are collecting microforms as fast or faster than book materials and recent statistics show Denver with 302,000, Milwaukee with one-half million, and Michigan with one million microforms. The hours of service are 96, 100, and 101 per week respectively. All have their microforms fully cataloged, with Michigan providing a catalog with main and subject entries and shelflist in the microform area. Michigan has also compiled an extensive workbook of its collection which helps in bibliographic and acquisition work as well as in servicing the collection. For the most part, indexes and reference tools remain in the Reference area, but some miscellaneous materials for use with the collection are housed in the microform area and Michigan State houses its *New York Times Index* there. At Denver lists showing materials in microform are placed next to the idexes shelved in the Reference area. Spreitzer reports a general trend toward sequential numbering of microforms rather than classification, using a separate series of numbers for each form. Both Michigan State and Denver follow this with Milwaukee using a very short form of the Library of Congress classification.

In staffing patterns the three libraries vary, but all have positively attuned staffs. Michigan State has a Librarian as department head, plus two full-time and one part-time workers with 85 hours per week of student assistance. Milwaukee's center is staffed with civil-service employees and student assistants, while Denver uses 93 hours of student help, the key assistant usually being a library school student responsible for keeping the reading equipment in good condition.

The lighting arrangement on the third floor facility at Michigan State shields the daylight with partitions. Ceiling lights are normally turned off, providing sufficient ambient light. At Milwaukee, fluorescent perimeter lighting supplemented by general lighting heightens the impression of light without increasing the ambient light. At Denver alternate rows of non-glare, recessed fluorescent lights can be turned off and on by a switch near the Service Desk.

Access to the collection is open at Michigan and Denver with re-shelving done by the staff, while Milwaukee has check out for room use at the Service Desk. The statistics show newspapers on microfilm a high-use item, as expected. Microfilm use runs more than two to one over microfiche, with ERIC accounting for eighty-three percent to one hundred percent of the fiche use. The statistics showing ratio of film to fiche can be expected to change in the future as more materials are available in the microfiche format.

The fourth library is at Martin Luther King Branch of the Sacramento City-County Library. Two thousand reels of microfilm in five film cabinets, a reader and a reader/printer are all centrally serviced, but not in close proximity. The collection on film contains Martin Luther King material and ten-year back-files of periodicals chosen from the *Readers' Guide*. The films are checked out one reel at a time and users are instructed in the use of the machines. The same care for users, materials and equipment exists in this small operation as in the larger ones previously described.

Spreitzer blames the "problem with microforms" in libraries not on inadequate equipment nor user resistance, but on the general ignorance of applied micrographics in libraries and the low position given microform users on the scale of library priorities. Better application of what is already known and what is already available on the market can greatly improve the microforms operations as shown in those cases he described. Assuming that the importance of a very good microform operation is as great as that of any other service area in the library, very good results from careful planning can be accomplished without extravagant costs.

In 1976 Marvin Guilfoyle made a study of microform practice and its possible application for the Bizzell Library of the University of Oklahoma.[15] A committee appointed by the Director to address the qùstion had determined (1) that microform use had become heavy, (2) that the materials scattered throughout the building caused problems of location, use-instruction, equipment maintenance, and storage, (3) Microform use would increase because of the greatly increasing output of the micropublishing industry, and (4) A change from present methods of storage and use was necessary to better serve the students and faculty of Oklahoma University. An area in which the microforms could be centrally housed and serviced would become available. In his study report, Guilfoyle recommended a closed stack area, with the area arranged so that the stacks could be opened if the need arose, even though it would require additional staffing. With the closed stack, he recommended using standard library shelving to hold films in their own containers or in acid-free boxes. Cabinets would be used for microfiche. Comparison of the number of readers and reader/printers used by several other libraries brought him to the conclusion that only experience would confirm or deny what a sufficient number for the Bizzell Library would be.

The library community does not appear to agree on the value of service contracts for machine maintenance, and so the Bizzell Library would experiment for one year without contracts, paying for repairs and keeping detailed records as a guide for a second year decision. This report discusses the possibilities of circulating microfiche and microfilm, probably making copies of the fiche available and some checking out of film to departments for use, but in general expresses the hope that the microform area would be so attractive and comfortable that there would be no wish to check out materials. The author considers the array of factors necessary to a well-run facility, including the promotion of the collection and the area, and suggests one additional come-on to lure the faculty. An adjoining room, not needed for storage at first, might be furnished comfortably as a faculty area with good reading machines and, of course, the inevitable coffee pot. Enthusiastic librarians, led by the Director, would persuade the faculty, and other users as well, to give the media a fair chance. By the time the room is needed for storage, the transformation to happy acceptance of the media will have occurred.

Whether a centralized or decentralized approach to collections and equipment is developed, there are likely to be other libraries in the system that have some holdings and equipment. There may also be teaching departments or other non-library areas housing some microforms. Anne Vandenbugh of the University of Wisconsin-Madison, which has over one hundred libraries and reading rooms, has designed a questionnaire for an inventory of microform holdings and equipment.[16] Because of the many reduction ratios in microform production, any one center may not have lenses available to accommodate all. Some areas may have time limits on use or other restrictions so that staff may wish to note the restricted-use on any public lists. At Wisconsin-Madison, charts were made of location and magnifications of readers and reader/printers for fiche and film, and copies distributed to respondents and to the staff of reference and information desks. A guide with detailed description of each center, its hours, restrictions, collections, and machine capability has been prepared as a handout for users. As Vandenburgh suggests, the survey could be used by consortia or other groups of libraries in an area where it may be desirable to provide broader access to existing collections and equipment.

Complete bibliographic control—the descriptive representation of every item in a collection, usually in catalog card form and supplemented with indexes, reading lists, or guides to particular collections—is the optimum condition for providing reader-access to information in microforms. In the past many libraries provided cataloging for collections, but depended on indexes or guides to locate individual items in the collections. While librarians urged, even demanded, that microform publishers provide cards that analyzed the collections, they could hardly refuse to purchase a valuable set for which no cards were provided. In some cases the publishers did not see this as their responsibility; in others, they were willing, but had no cataloging staff available to prepare the cards. In those cases where cards were offered, the prices were so high that a library could afford only one card for each title and had duplicates made in the library or by a commercial firm at less than the purchase price of the full set. Cards offered, free or for a sum, could have outdated entries and subject headings so that revisions would be necessary on the one card before it was reproduced, or on the full set of cards.

An index to a collection, while extremely useful once you know the set is on the premises, is useless to the person who does not know that the set is in the library and cannot guess which titles may be found in it. In the past, microforms have not received high priority treatment partly because of the time and expense of cataloging large collections and the resulting expansion of the card catalog. In addition, the titles were frequently old and seemingly less in demand by users than the newer titles in hard copy. It was easy to delay cataloging especially when there was available a printed bibliography, index, or finding list of some sort. The difference in attitude of catalogers in eagerness to prepare the description for books and for microforms may be caused by the physical evidence of accomplishment. A truck of books cataloged and on the way to shelf-preparation and the stacks is far more heartening evidence of work completed than a few reels of microfilm or a packet of microfiche occupying a few square inches on a truck or in a manila envelope. The mind-set needed for working happily for days with small amounts of film or fiche must be developed from appreciation of the value of the material contained and the real service provided the seeker of the information. In some libraries the increase in use of a set after it has been fully cataloged has been sufficient to overcome initial resistance and to encourage the cataloger to greet the next collection with some enthusiasm. Most libraries with large collections are now making efforts to provide cataloging, through commercial offerings at extra cost or through in-house preparation. The University of Michigan has offered its cataloging of microforms for sale to defray some of the expenses of its efforts. Had timing been better between the acquisition of large collections and the availability of shared cataloging by contributors to data bases, the assignments for cataloging sets or parts of sets could have been made through networks to individual libraries. New collections may well be done in this way in the future with some later plan for keying in the retrospective titles, a mind-boggling consideration in the light of where we may be going with or after the card catalog.

In addition to the publication *Microform Review,* which has provided comprehensive reviews of many microform collections since 1972, Microform, Inc. is responsible for the important tools in selecting for purchase or identifying titles: *Guide to Microform in Print, Subject Guide to Microforms in Print* and the quarterly update to these—*Microlist, Micropublishers' Trade List Annual,* and *Microform Market Place.* The *National Register of Microform Masters,* begun in 1965 by the Library of Congress to encourage the preservation of texts, lists library materials filmed for which master negatives exist and where, and has now become an acquisitions tool. *Newspapers in Microform: United States: 1948–1972* and its companion volume for foreign countries provide a union list of holdings of newspapers in various microforms reported by libraries. Suzanne Dodson's *Microform Research Collections: A Guide* provides easier access to titles in some 200 large microform collections offered by American and European micropublishers. Full information is given, including access tools available in the form of catalog cards or reel guides, associated indexes and bibliographies, exisiting reviews and format notes, and the content and scope of each unit. This guide could be annotated to show the holdings in a particular library. While the tools mentioned and local listings are extremely useful and may serve as bibliographical control for some time yet, full cataloging is still an ideal to be pursued. With cooperative and coordinated effort, libraries may be able to apportion the input of records into data bases for COM or on-line access to microforms in the future.

With regard to conservation and preservation, microfilm may be viewed in two aspects: the care and preservation of the film itself, and the film as a medium for preserving other documents. Most libraries clean film "as needed," but few have any regular program reports Nancy Knight.[17] She recommends an inspection program to reveal whether cleaning is necessary, what kinds of dirt are present, the condition of the film in relation to repair of splices, brittleness of film, and whether film is scratched. The four methods of cleaning recommended are: (1) Wiping with a dry cloth or soft brush (2) Wiping with a cloth or brush moistened with cleaning solvent (3) Cleaning with ionized air—a mechanical device blasts air across film to dislodge dust and lint and then vacuums it away (4) Cleaning with ultrasonic frequencies, by machines which dry clean or use solvents. As may be expected the fourth method is considered the best, but it is the most expensive. Cleaning machines using one or more of the methods recommended cost from around $700 to $10,000. In her guidelines for cleaning, Knight recommends care in the choice of cleaning materials: cloth that is absorbent and lint-free, solvents that are safe for the environment and used in a properly ventilated area, solvent containers that are tightly closed and small enough to keep evaporation at a minimum. Film should be dry when it is wound on the take-up reel; when re-wound, sufficient tension must be exerted to produce a tight roll, but not so tight as to cause scratches. Clean reading rooms, well dusted and vacuumed, and clean equipment, especially those parts which come in contact with the film, will reduce the need for cleaning the film itself. Containers that protect the film and care in handling, proper temperature control, and relative humidity in the film storage and use area should keep the film in good and stable condition.

As expected, the use of film for preservation of books and documents has met with most resistance from scholars who wish to study and handle the original. If the original is a manuscript or a particularly beautiful example of printing, paper, or binding or is valuable as an association copy, that is, important as a physical object, it may be required for use by the scholar in its original form. However, if this physical object is filmed for use by those who are primarily interested in its intellectual content, the original will survive longer to be made available to scholars for their particular study. The purpose for which material is sought and used must determine the form or forms in which it is preserved. Repairing and rebinding current materials to last for the period of their high use may be the best decision. Restoration, however, is another and very expensive matter, and should be reserved for rare and special materials. Pamela Darling in her *Developing a Preservation Microfilming Program* uses the figure of "a dollar a page to de-acidify, laminate and rebind."[18] The library must determine very carefully how it wishes to use its funds to the best advantage for the services which it performs. Crowded shelves make books harder to find and encourage misshelving, replacing a book in any space that's vacant and nearby, or laying it on top of others. Squeezing books into tight shelf spaces can damage bindings and loosen hinges while retrieving them can rip spines and may even result in damage to the shelver. Replacing some items with microform frees needed shelf space. Little-used backfiles of periodicals become good candidates for microform replacement, retaining only the current year in paper or the most recent five or ten years, as deemed necessary for expected use. Where there are duplicate serials, one file may be committed to microform and if a library still holds paper copies of newspapers they would be a first for replacement. Documents, technical reports, unbound pamphlets, and any deteriorating materials are among the appropriate categories.

Darling urges determining a policy, developing guidelines, and providing for implementation as precisely as possible. Categories to be purchased on film in the first place, materials received in poor condition that should be transferred to film quickly, and disintegrating materials in the stacks to be replaced, should be included in the policy so that a balance can be maintained in the treatment of old and new items. Efforts to avoid perpetuating the bibliomaniac sins of the past by considering the condition and microform appropriateness of current acquisitions will reap their rewards in the future state of the collection. Selection officers, receivers, shelf-preparers, indeed, staff members throughout the library, should be aware of the microform policy and their particular responsibilities in carrying it out. Part of the policy will be the exceptions known currently and others which may become obvious in the collection of a particular library or in the special use of particular information. There are materials not appropriate to microform (in its present state and use) such as music scores used for performing. Others, such as statistical tables or mathematical formulae viewed for purposes of comparison, are awkward to use in microform. Works important largely or solely for plates or other illustration are not satisfactory in black and white, but may be very useful in color. This leads to the consideration of two other important factors (1) the appropriateness of film, fiche, or micro-opaques in which reduction for what kinds of material and (2) the quality of the microform commecially available.

In procuring microforms, the least expensive method is to purchase commercially-produced items. If the work sought is not available, the library may send its copy to be filmed. This must be done with great care and attention given to choosing a vendor, detailing the specifications, monitoring test results, and inspecting closely the final product. With some micropublishers, it is possible to have a microform copy made in return for the loan of the library's original if the publisher wants to offer the film for sale. A warning is in order here against entrusting materials to individuals who offer film in return for their loan. The library must make sure that this is a legitimate enterprise or it may never see either its materials or the film again. The least appealing method of obtaining film, for most libraries, is to film the material on the premises. This is not a realistic solution unless the library or its parent institution has already established facilities or intends to inaugurate an ongoing program. Darling warns that "the same sort of careful analysis and program development that is essential for automation is needed to establish a feasible preservation microfilming program. The technology is not as complex, of course, but it demands respect and attention to detail, both technical and bibliographic. . . . If we take time to learn what it's all about and make the technology work to meet our needs, we may yet save the millions of volumes which will otherwise crumble to dust on our shelves before this century is over."[19]

In the past few years librarians have come to realize that the elements in the environment that are uncomfortable or that do actual harm to people have also done damage to printed materials. Air pollution, temperature, dampness or dry heat, dust, insects, daylight, and some artificial lighting are severe enemies.

Add to these the disrespect with which books have been treated even by those who profess to give them tender loving care. Normal handling by people will take its toll in time, but the physical contaminants that people add to printed materials—rubber bands, paper clips, acid paper inserts, pressure sensitive tapes, to say nothing of flowers pressed between pages and odd items put in to hold the reader's place such as dollar bills and strips of bacon—all contribute to damage, occasionally irretrievable. Even the glues and paper materials used in repairing may have run a close second to molds and mildew in hastening the end of a popular volume. As has been mentioned before, keeping stack storage areas clean and controlling temperature and humidity can help to retard further damage. Air scrubbers in the heating/cooling system, and the use of plastic sleeves to filter fluorescent light, can improve the book environment greatly. But to attempt to preserve and restore every title in the collection is not economically nor physically feasible. Restoration methods may become less time-consuming and less expensive in the future when books can be treated and de-acidified in quantity. In the meantime, a balanced program of committing titles to microform, restoring some and rebinding or repairing others carefully should be instituted. The combination of in-house and commercial services must depend on staff skills and the facilities available to the given library. There are regional conservation and preservation services developing, some non-profit, as the New England Document Conservation Center. In addition there are existing and proposed consortial arrangements for preservation which consider a microfilming preservation program an integral part of their activities.

No discussion of preservation can omit some comments on the controversy that continues about the types of film available and their uses—silver halide, diazo, and vesicular. The controversy was given a good workout in the December 1978 issue of *American Libraries*. Led by Carl M. Spaulding's article "Kicking the Silver Habit: Confessions of a Former Addict" presenting his case for the reconsidered use of the three types, a mini-symposium of statements from seven other experts in the field followed.[20]

Silver halide is exposed by the photochemical effect of visible light on certain silver compounds held in a gelatin emulsion on the surface of the film and developed very carefully in a darkroom in chemical baths and water rinses. Diazo and vesicular film are exposed by ultraviolet light; diazo is developed by ammonia, interacting with diazonium salts in the film to produce deeply colored dye images. Vesicular film is developed by heat to bring out images in the form of microscopic bubbles or vesicles which diffract light and produce the same visual effect as opaque areas on other types of film. ANSI (American National Standards Institute) has set silver halide film standards and declared it (if processed, stored, and handled correctly) to be archival film suitable for records having permanent value. The repeated caution is, however, that the archival quality of silver halide film is maintained only when the processing is archival and the storage conditions are as recommended. The silver film costs more and is not necessary for material that will be replaced, such as Computer Output Microform or other microform services whose parts are updated over a period of time. Master negative film must be preserved and archival silver film is appropriate for that purpose. However, Spaulding recommends that the library community work with micropublishers on procedures to insure "that the latter are producing camera and print master films which meet archival standards and are storing and handling them in accordance with the ANSI standard. The importance of such an arrangement cannot be overstated, for it is the micropublisher's master film, not print film in library collections, which is true archival copy."[21]

Returning to the microform facility as it represents a complete program, there are two libraries whose plans and ongoing implementation should be detailed: those at Princeton University and at Boston University.

In 1976 Princeton University began a comprehensive program to improve its microform services. From a basement area housing a variety of poorly maintained equipment with no professional staff to supervise or provide reference help, the service was moved to quarters adjoining the main entrance to the library. New equipment was purchased, reader/printers transferred from the photoduplication area, and a grant obtained for cataloging the microform backlog and for completely cataloging the microform sets. The University budget provided a salary for a new professional head of the division.[22]

To influence public opinion, Princeton initiated a two-part campaign to persuade users and staff that conversion to microforms could simplify and improve library services as well as increase the library's purchasing power. A grant from the Council on Library Resources was obtained to support the training of the microform division staff and an orientation program to instruct students and faculty in microform use and availability. The program included a seminar, for librarians in the surrounding area as well as for the Princeton staff, at which authorities in micrographics presented the essential topics of microform sources, organization, storage, retrieval, and equipment. As a second step, acquisition of microforms would be in stages, each to prepare users and staff to accept the next stage. Areas where the advantage of microform was fairly obvious, such as corporate annual reports, telephone and city directories, statistical documents, would be first choices. Second-stage candidates were those periodical titles whose issues most often disappeared or were mutilated. Emphasis on the service advantage in these first stages should prepare the users to accept readily further journal backfiles and other materials.

The Princeton plan seems ideal, combining effort in physical improvements, training program for staff and users, and economic considerations, with first and continued focus on service. It should certainly serve as a guide to those contemplating redoing the old microform program or establishing a new one. The emphasis on preparation for "adjustment to change" as an important psychological factor in user and staff acceptance of anything new must not be ignored, especially in an area where preconceived notions exist, as they do with regard to microforms. Even libraries which may not have planned as much time as Princeton to set the stage for the new service must be aware of its importance and include education for change as a part of their programs.

At Boston University, the Mugar Memorial library opened in 1966 as a central library for the university community. At an earlier period, some thirteen separate libraries existed to serve the various schools and departments, the largest being that of the College of Liberal Arts which became the nucleus of the central library. The libraries for Law, Medicine, and Theology continued as separate facilities.

The library had accumulated some microform titles and collections in addition to the Boston University dissertations. A microform area of 846 square feet was provided on the third floor. Eight readers and one reader/printer were housed with 940 microfilm titles and 2,700 micro-opaque titles on forty-one sections of shelving. Student assistants were available in the area for forty-two hours per week. In 1970 the microform collection and needed equipment had outgrown its area at about the same time that its area was needed by the adjacent Catalog Department. Terminals for on-line cataloging and the shelving for cataloging tools and materials being worked on would need space so that changes in work flow procedures could be accomplished efficiently.

Microforms were moved to an area below ground level, a basement room at the front of the building with 2,658 square feet of space, but with no claim to aesthetic satisfaction. From the elevator at the basement level, the approach to the room was through a doorway and down a ramp with pipe-like hand-holds as a balustrade. The space for microforms surrounded a square, locked vault used for some Special Collections materials. The high ceiling had fluorescent drop lights. Exposed pipes and utility conveyors ran hither and yon. White paint on the walls and linoleum tile on the floor rounded out an undistinguished area. This Microform Reading Room became the responsibility of the Serials/Processing/Microforms Department, not an unusual alliance since many microforms are serial in nature. The person in charge of the area became knowledgeable of the collection and the equipment and could make replacements and minor repairs. Service was available for sixty-seven staffed hours in 1970/71 and seventy-three in 1971/72.

As additional materials became available in microform, especially back runs of periodicals, a program developed to complete hard copy runs, to substitute microform for hard copy, and to purchase back runs or fill-ins new to the library's collection. Second copies were replaced by microfilm as back ups and in some cases only the most recent one, five, or ten years were kept in paper with full runs in microform. The primary advantages of the program were: (1) to provide one or more complete files where several volumes were missing or where issues had been removed from volumes, and/or where paper or binding had deteriorated and (2) to release some badly needed shelving space.

Microform and equipment providers suggested special offers on bulk purchases and gave advice on rearranging the old equipment and placing the new to increase the housing capacity and save floor space at the same time. With some general departmental reorganization in the library, Microforms became a part of the Reference Department, located on the first floor, so that closer communication and responsibility for information search and dispersal could develop between the two areas. Microforms, too, became part of the student orientation tours and sessions, with an information sheet prepared for distribution to users. The variety of indexing and abstracting services and the increasing number of available reference tools makes it very important to provide extensive instruction to users in academic libraries. Students' experiences in libraries before college are very uneven, in some cases non-existent, in having searched for information themselves and in having developed skills in the use of some tools. Faculty members, too, need to be updated and kept apprised of the newer library services. Group instruction is the most economic and time-saving method and has the additional advantage of interaction of questions and comments posed by members of the group. Otherwise, instruction, if provided at all, must be given on an individual basis frequently hurried and incomplete, thus subject to repetition the next time the student has a question. Microforms, essential elements in the library's services, must become an integral part of library instruction.

A word of caution in relation to the disposition of paper copies when they are replaced by microforms should be included here. Visible discard of large amounts of material will be greeted by cries of outrage from those to whom the printed word is sacred and those whose concern for the world's needy includes the distribution of reading material, wanted or not. Possible uses of this material would be commercial sale, offering material to other library members of your consortium or to the library-sponsored book sales, offering some appropriate back-files to faculty members, or sending materials to USBE (Universal Serial and Book Exchange) according to its guidelines. Other options may suggest themselves, depending on the material.

Another warning is in order with regard to consulting with faculty to make sure that there is reasonable agreement as to length of time to retain hard copy backfiles if at all, the suitability of microform for certain material in their subject areas, and in some cases, the disposition of the hard copies. There will be some problems even when the library has been extremely conscientious in these matters, but it is desirable to keep them as few as possible. It is wise not to let the pressure of vendors' deadlines for decisions on bulk purchases force less than adequate time for consideration of the users and the materials selected. At the same time, the vendors' representatives may have constraints on them which the librarian should appreciate and work around, the position of arbitrator not being an entirely unfamiliar one to librarians. The other half of the acquisition coin turns up when the material arrives. Receiving large orders of microforms, especially periodical backfiles, will probably require a painstaking system of check in. Film boxes may have insufficient or incorrect labels and shippers' carelessness in boxing materials may divide titles into several shipments to provide a complete run. Invoices, not always the essence of clarity, may not be helpful in untangling the puzzle. Serials receivers, however, forewarned of these possibilities, will respond with their usual vigilance.

By the summer of 1977, Boston University had made a decision to expand its microform services again. Although some colorful wall hangings had been added in the microform area and some extra pieces of carpet adorned the floor, it was clear that major refurbishing would be needed to make the area attractive, comfortable, and thus inviting. A three-stage plan for equipment and redecorating was proposed by a microform provider. The library decided to go for the full plan, to be accomplished during the summer. Since the equipment and materials had to be moved out for the physical changes in the area, one large disturbance completed in a reasonable length of time would be preferable to three separate ones over some three-year period. Too, the dramatic effect of the complete changeover would be more useful in encouraging students and faculty to take the service seriously and appreciatively since the library obviously considered it so important. The construction and decoration would be done by the university's Building and Grounds' Department at less cost than by outside contracting.

Some changes from the original plans were made, but the results have proven satisfactory.

Several alternatives for temporary relocation of the service were proposed and examined by the staff members concerned. The third floor rear of the building offered the best solution. Normally a study area, the carrels and tables there could be used for materials and equipment. There were enough shelves available for indexes, but others would have had to be emptied and books relocated had the carrels not been used for housing microfilm in call number order. Tables were used for some material and for reading machines. With a smaller user population in the summer, some equipment could be stored elsewhere along with the lesser-used microforms that could easily be paged upon request. Storage cabinets were lined up and tables arranged to isolate the area from general library traffic. Additional student help provided paging and any other coverage needed for satisfactory service in this area. Service was suspended for four days in May, during intersession, when the move to the temporary location took place. Ample directional signs steered users to the new area and service resumed without apparent inconvenience to the public.

In the meantime, redecoration went forward apace. The walls were covered with vinyl-coated gypsum board and painted a pale "almond paste." Acoustic panels in muted browns, rust, orange, and sand were applied to the walls. The ramp railing was boxed in and covered with a golden brown carpeting and some 328 square yards of brown-tweed mixture carpeting were installed on the ramp and over the entire floor area. Two levels of handholds were installed along the side of the ramp—one at walking height, the other for wheel chair users. A coat and hat storage rack was placed on the upper ramp level to the left of the entrance to the Microform Library. An acoustic tile ceiling was suspended to eight feet above the floor and was fixed with recessed lighting. Four foot fluorescent fixtures around the walls of the vault serve as wall washers (light reflects off the wall) for general lighting and down lights (recessed bulb directs light downward) for concentrated illumination. Fire sensors were affixed to the ceiling and a smoke detector installed near the entrance. A work room for service and repair was fully enclosed in a corner of the area and provided with a secure door. The room is equipped with a sink, storage cabinets for replacement parts, supplies such as toner and paper for the copying machines, and cleaning and splicing materials. The microfiche duplicating machine with its appurtenances is also housed here.

Additional readers were purchased to bring the total up to ten microfiche, one ultrafiche, four micro-opaque, and thirty-eight motorized microfilm reading machines. There are two reader/printers and one fiche-to-fiche copier. Also available is an X-Pert Visual Aid machine which enlarges print for the use of the visually handicapped. Some reading machines have been modified to accommodate the manually handicapped.

To house the readers, forty-two carrels (36 × 36 × 51 inch) were installed for the microfilm readers and sixteen carrels (24 × 36 × 51 inch) for the microfiche, ultrafiche, and micro-opaque readers. It may be useful to point out that while a free-standing carrel requires two end supports, two carrels side by side will save the space of one end piece, five lined up will save four end pieces, etc. Metal conduits bringing electric lines down from the ceiling were inconspicuously placed behind the carrels to supply the extra outlets needed for the new machines.

Black storage cabinets were added, bringing the total for reel storage to thirty, each housing 35,760 reels of 35mm film, more of 16mm. Twenty-one microfiche cabinets, with a filing capacity of 16,000 each, house 336,000 fiche. Ultrafiche have separate file trays as does the College Catalog collection. Forty-eight sections of shelving contain the boxed 6 × 9 inch micro-opaques and another eight sections hold the indexes, finding lists, and bibliographies. When the shelving was returned to the new area, the end caps were painted a golden brown or butterscotch shade.

The collection, now over a million volumes, has sufficient housing with some room for expansion, but early dissertations, a music manuscript collection, and the Human Relations Area Files are stored in the sub-basement level near the elevator, for easy paging. A service desk area was built out from the wall of the center vault, near the lower end of the ramp, with work space and comfortable chairs for two staff members. Lounge seating for several waiting users is available, but only infrequently used.

The existing heating/cooling system was considered appropriate for the materials in the area, but it must be monitored for any sudden variation in temperature or humidity so that corrections can be made as soon as possible.

Cataloging has been completed (but not all the filing of the limitless number of cards) for most of the larger collections. Some smaller collections not cataloged can be used with the indexes and finding tools available, but the increased use of materials after cataloging has been sufficiently impressive to urge the continued emphasis on cataloging as much of the material as possible. These cards appear in the main catalogs on the first floor. Microfilms and the 6 × 9 inch micro-opaques have been classified. In the Microform Library there is a visible index giving the call numbers for microfilm periodicals and collections, and for micro-opaque serial sets and collections. The microfiche are arranged alphabetically by entry of item or set, and then by internal code number or year and volume, as appropriate to the item. As time passes and as the microfiche collection enlarges, it may be necessary to assign a sequential numbering system, not necessarily a classification system, to microfiche for finding purposes.

Two full-time library technicians and 100 hours of student help cover the Microform Library for 101 hours per week. The senior member has had experience at the Reference Desk and trains the student workers in the Microform Library not only on the materials there, but also on which materials or kinds of information should be referred to the Reference area. All are trained in the general care of the machines and replacement of parts.

Users are assisted in finding materials or using equipment as needed and are requested to return materials to a book truck for re-shelving or refiling by staff. Film is cleaned as needed with a soft cloth, a solvent added if necessary.

Reaction to the new facility has been very positive. Attendants at the Reference Desk report that only infrequently are there unhappy expressions when the user is directed to the Microform Library. This does not mean that the operation is perfect. There have been some complaints about the lighting, which can be partly a matter of personal preference just as room temperature is, but revisions have been made in bulb size or shape and other refinements may be required in the future. More direc-

Figure 13

Microform Library
Mugar Memorial Library Boston University

Before Renovation

Figure 14

Microform Library
Mugar Memorial Library Boston University

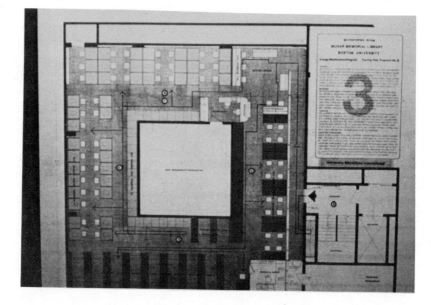

After Renovation

Figure 15

Microform Library
Mugar Memorial Library Boston University

After Renovation

tional signs may be useful and a map of the area showing location of the various collections is being produced to be posted at
several locations in the room with a "you are here" symbol. A
glassed-in exhibit case is planned for the wall space to the left of
the entrance for notices of new acquisitions or other small displays.

It may be soon desirable to add another copier or to install
several coin-operated machines. The subject of copying machines requires some remarks on the revised copyright law. A
"Display Warning of Copyright" must be posted at the place
where orders for copies are accepted or where patrons use coin-
operated copiers. Attendants who make copies must be familiar
with and follow the "fair use" guidelines. "Order Warning of
Copyright" has to be included on printed forms supplied by
libraries and used by patrons for ordering copies. Both warn-
ings consist of the verbatim statement:

> NOTICE! The copyright law of the United States "Title 17, U.S. Code"
> governs the making of photocopies or other reproductions of copyright
> material.
>
> Under certain conditions specified in the law, libraries and archives are
> authorized to furnish a photocopy or other reproduction. One of these
> specified conditions is that the photocopy or reproduction is not used
> for any purpose other than private study, scholarship, or research. If a
> user makes a request for, or later uses, a photocopy or reproduction for
> purposes in excess of "fair use," that user may be liable for copyright
> infringement.
>
> This institution reserves the right to refuse to accept a copying order if,
> in its judgement, fulfillment of the order would involve violation of the
> copyright law.[23]

Additional information is available from the Copyright Office
at the Library of Congress and the November 1976 issue of
American Libraries has three very useful articles on the copyright
law of January 1978.[24]

Use statistics are taken by person count only and show a ten
percent increase, to 22,000 per year, since the new facility
opened. The increase might have been more dramatic had not
one service previously provided, the storage of paper copies of
newspapers, been removed to another location. With increased
library instruction, more materials represented in the catalog,

and other efforts at advertising the microform service, further expansion of use can be expected.

On the first floor of the library there is a user "Suggestion Box," with a bulletin board, for user notes and librarians' replies. The most extensive note, with a signature, on reactions to the Microform Library read:

Sir:

This is a formal complaint opposing the renovation of the microfilm room. Not only have you improved the lighting, used the space to its maximum by re-arranging the machines but you had the gall to paint the front of the bookcases.

I find these actions revolting since they have given professors crazy ideas such as the microfilm room should be used more often. And since I am using the microfilm more, I can't make the old complaints hold water. My eyes don't squint as I search for an issue of the Atlantic Monthly. More machines means I have to look at the film.

Basically the final question is as follows:

Are you trying to make college enjoyable? If you are, then you are going against the general policy of education.

The importance of the Boston University facility is that it serves as an example of what can be done with a seemingly impossible area. Location on the first floor adjacent to the Reference area would have been better, but buildings in urban areas go up in the air with limited floor space rather than being spread across the landscape. All the good and desirable services that must vie with each other for first floor or entry level space simply cannot be accommodated.

Perhaps a comment, though obvious, should be made about the importance of the Microform area staff being familiar with the Reference collection as well as the Reference Staff with the Microform collection, and of course, with the various other services the library provides. Users who are satisfied with the information they find in the Reference area and have worked with particular staff members are much inclined to return to the scene of their success, frequently to seek out the persons who assisted them. The same is true in the Microform area, with users going directly there with high expectations of finding everything they need. The same guidance and concern for the user's needs should be provided by the Microform staff as by the Reference people. Microform and Reference services must be extensions of each other.

On the occasion of the Microform Library Opening at Boston University, W. Carl Jackson, Dean of Indiana University Libraries, spoke on *Bibliographic Access to Microforms: On the Threshold?*[25] He called for a national office for microforms to coordinate programs including a national cataloging plan, and spoke of a meeting of library leaders who expressed and supported the elements of a national strategy to include microforms in the developing national bibliographic structure:

1. To broaden the MARC format to include the access points necessary for microforms.
2. To include those revisions necessary for microforms in the manual of bibliographic conventions for automated library networks.
3. To identify a means for micropublishers to input their cataloging into the national bibliographic network without financial loss.
4. To include microforms in the programs to teach librarians the changes necessary for implementation of AACR II.
5. To develop a standard for commercial bibliographic listings of microforms.[26]

The Association of Research Libraries, in the Spring of 1979, applied for a grant to support a one-year project designed to improve the bibliographic control of microforms. Librarians, micropublishers, and others would develop means for the cooperative creation and dissemination of cataloging records after assessing the current state of bibliographic control and setting priorities for attack on the identified problems. Specifications for the decentralized creation of nationally-acceptable, machine-readable records for microform sets would allow and encourage shared responsibility among librarians and micropublishers for creating and distributing bibliographic tools for microform materials. The planning would be related to current projects at the Library of Congress, the Council on Library Resources, and elsewhere concerned with providing national bibliographical services.[27] Jackson noted that improved bibliographic access would enhance the value of microform collections, users could easily discover the richness of the materials, and the increased use that would follow would put a strain on libraries to improve staffing, equipment, and facilities.

Indeed, even those who already have new or revised facilities could feel such a strain. Although microforms come in small packages, those packages increase rapidly with all the good materials that micropublishers can think of to put in them—constant temptations to libraries to enrich their resources. But it must be remembered that they do require space and that the space must provide an environment congenial to their care and preservation and congenial to those who use them—including, of course, the staffing service—to insure optimum use and care of machines and equipment. The end of the microform revolution is not yet in sight. Weapons, strategy, and tactics may change in the future, but the intelligence will still be sought and must be provided.

NOTES

1. Veaner, Allen B. "Micropublications," *Advances in Librarianship* 2 (1971): 165–186.

2. Association of Research Libraries, *Academic Library Statistics 1969/70* (Washington: Association of Research Libraries, 1970).

3. Association of Research Libraries, *ARL Statistics 1977/78* (Washington: Association of Research Libraries, 1978).

4. Prevel, James. *Microform Environment Microform Utilization: The Academic Library Environment,* Report of a Conference held at Denver, Colorado, 7–9 December, 1971, p. 144.

5. Holmes, Donald C. *Determination of User Needs and Future Requirements for a Systems Approach to Microform Technology* (Washington: Association of Research Libraries, 1969), (ED 029-168).

6. *Library Technology Reports,* (Microforms and Equipment Sections P. P1. P2), 1965–75 and September 1976 and March 1977 issues.

7. *Micrographics Equipment Review* (Weston, Connecticut: Microform Review, Inc.), v. 1– , Jan. 1976– .

8. Ballou, Hubbard W. ed. *Guide to Microreproduction Equipment,* 6th ed. (Silver Springs, Maryland: National Microfilm Association, 1975).

9. Holmes, Donald C. *Determination of the Environmental Conditions Required in a Library for the Effective Utilization of Microforms* (Washington: Association of Research Libraries, 1970), (ED-046-403), p. 12.

10. Tannenbaum, Arthur and Sidhom, Eva. "User Environment and Attitudes in an Academic Microform Center," *Library Journal* 101 (October 15, 1976): 2140.

11. Ibid.
12. Ibid., p. 2141.
13. Ibid., pp. 2142–43.
14. Spreitzer, Francis. "Library Microform Facilities," *Library Technology Reports* 12 (July 1976): 407–35.
15. Guilfoyle, Marvin C. *Microform Centralization Project: A Survey of Current Practice and Possible Application in Bizzell Library.* A report to the Director of Libraries (Norman, Oklahoma: Oklahoma University Library, 1976), (ED 122-785).
16. Vandenburgh, Anne. "Inventory of Microform Centers on a Major University Campus," *Microform Review* 7 (November 1978): 317–320.
17. Knight, Nancy H. "The Cleaning of Microforms, *Library Technology Reports* 14 (May/June 1978): 217–240.
18. Darling, Pamela W. "Developing a Preservation Microfilming Program," *Library Journal* 99 (November 1, 1974): 2803–9.
19. Ibid., pp. 2808–2809.
20. Spaulding, Carl M. "Kicking the Silver Habit: Confessions of a Former Addict," *American Libraries* 9 (December, 1978): 653–56; 665–69.
21. Ibid., p. 665.
22. "Princeton Microfilm Project," *Association of Research Libraries Newsletter* no. 84 (December 1976): 6–7.
23. U.S. Copyright Office, "Reproduction of Copyrighted Works by Educators and Librarians," *Circular R21* (1978), p. 24.
24. "Librarians Weigh New Copyright Law Effective January 1978," *American Libraries* 7 (November 1976): 609; "New Rules on Photocopy Limits and Classroom Use Set Forth in Full Text of Copyright Addenda," *American Libraries* 7 (November 1976): 610–611; "Do's and Don't's of Photocopying," *American Libraries* 7 (November 1976): 606.
25. Jackson, W. Carl. *Bibliographic Access to Microforms: On the Threshold?* Presented at Boston University May 10, 1978, pp. 9–10.
26. "Organizatonal Document: Planning Meeting on Establishing a Strategy for Bibliographic Control of Microforms," (Dated April 7, 1978), cited by W. Carl Jackson, *Bibliographic Access to Microforms: On the Threshold?* p. 10.
27. "ARL Seeks Grant to Improve Bibliographic Control of Microforms," *Association of Research Libraries Newsletter,* no. 96 (April 1979): 8.

BIBLIOGRAPHY

American Library Association, Bookdealer-Library Relations Committee. *Guidelines for Handling Library Orders for Microforms,* Acquisitions Guidelines No. 3. Chicago: ALA, 1977.

American Library Association, Library Standards for Microfilm Committee of the Copying Methods Section. *Microfilm Norms.* Chicago, ALA Resources and Technical Services Division, 1966.

Boss, Richard W. "Putting the Horse Before the Cart." *Microform Review* 7 (March/April 1978): 78–80.

Carroll, C. Edward. "Bibliographic Control of Microforms: Where do we go from Here?" *Microform Review* 7 (November 1978): 321–26).

Cluff, E. Dale. "Developments in Copying, Micrographics, and Graphic Communications, 1977. *Library Resources and Technical Services* 22 (Summer 1978): 263–93.

Cohen, Judy. "Microform Reader Printers for Libraries—A Survey." *Library Technology Reports* 12 (July 1976): 437–449.

Darling, Pamela W. "Developing a Preservation Microfilming Program." *Library Journal* 99 (November 1, 1974): 2803–9.

Dissertations Abstracts International, Vol. 1– , 1938– . Ann Arbor, Michigan: University Microfilms.

Dodson, Suzanne. *Microform Research Collections: A Guide.* Westport, Connecticut: Microform Review, 1978.

Fair, Judy. "Microtext Reading Room: A Practical Approach." *Microform Review,* 1 (July 1972): 199–202; 1 (October 1972): 269–73; 2 (January 1973): 9–13; 2 (July 1973): 168–71; 3 (January 1974): 11–14.

Farber, Evan I. "The Administration and Use of Microform Serials in College Libraries." *Microform Reiew* 7 (March/April 1978): 81–84.

Guide to Microforms in Print, 1961– . Washington, Microcard Editions.

Guide to Micrographic Equiment. 6th ed. Vol. 1. Silver Spring, Maryland: National Microfilm Association, 1975.

Guilfoyle, Marvin C. *Microform Centralization Project: A Survey of Current Practice and Possible Application in Bizzell Library,* A Report to the Director of Libraries. Norman, Oklahoma: Oklahoma University Library, 1976. (ED 122-785)

Hawken, William R. *Copying Methods Manual.* Chicago: Library Technology Program, American Library Association, 1966.

Hawken, William R. *Evaluating Microfiche Readers: A Handbook for Librarians.* Washington, Council on Library Resoruces, 1975.

Holmes, Donald C. *Determination of the Environmental Condition Required in a Library for the Effective Utilization of Microforms.* Washington: Association of Researach Li braries, 1970. (ED 046-403)

Journal of Micrographics, vol. 1– , Fall, 1967– . Silver Springs, Maryland: National Microfilm Association.

Knight, Nancy H. "The Cleaning of Microforms." *Library Technology Reports* 14 (May/June 1978): 217–240.

Kottenstette, James P. *An Investigation of the Characteristics of Ultrafiche and its Application to Colleges and Universities.* Denver: University of Denver, 1969. Final Report. (ED 032-447)

La Hood, Charles G. and Sullivan, Robert C. *Reprographic Services in Libraries: Organization and Administration.* Chicago: Library Technology Program, American Library Association, 1975.

Library Resources and Technical Services, vol. 16, no. 2–; Spring 1972– . Chicago: American Library Association. (Spring or Summer issues each year report the year's work in micrographics, its literature and products.)

Library Technology Reports. 1965– . Chicago: American Library Association. (Microforms and Equipment Sections P, P1, P2 1965–1975; September 1976, March 1977)

Martin, Murray S. "Promoting Microforms to Students and Faculty." *Microform Review* 8 (Spring 1979): 87–91.

A Microcourse in Microforms. Ann Arbor, Michigan: University Microfilms International, 1978. (16mm color cartridge sound-filmstrip and 4-page guide)

Microform Review, vol. 1– , Jan. 1972– . Weston, Connecticut: Microform Review, Inc.

Micrographics Equipment Review, vol. 1– , January/July 1976– . Weston, Connecticut: Microform Review, Inc.

Napier, Paul A. "Developments in Copying, Micrographics, and Graphic Communications, 1976." *Library Resources and Technical Services* 21 (Summer 1977): 187–215.

National Microfilm Association. *Buyer's Guide to Microfilm Equipment, Products and Services,* 1971– . Silver Spring, Maryland.

———. *How to Select a Reader or Reader/Printer.* Silver Spring, Maryland, 1974.

———. *Introduction to Micrographics.* Silver Spring, Maryland, 1973.

National Register of Microform Masters. 1965– . Washington: Library of Congress.

National Union Catalog of Manuscript Collections, 1959/61– . Washington: Library of Congress.

Newspaper and Gazette Report, vol. 1– , 1973– . Washington: Library of Congress.

Newspapers in Microform, 1973– . Washington: Library of Congress.

Nitecki, Joseph Z. *Directory of Library Reprographic Services: A World Guide.* Weston, Connecticut: Published for the Reproduction of Library Materials Section, RTSD—American Library Association by Microform Review, 1976.

Nutter, Susan. "Microforms and the User: Key Variable of User Acceptance in a Library Environment." *Drexel Library Quarterly* 11 (October, 1975): 17–31.

Prevel, James. *Microform Environment, Microform Utilization: The Academic Library Environment.* Report of a Conference held at Denver, Colorado, 7–9 December, 1971.

"Princeton Microfilm Project." *Association of Research Libraries Newsletter* 84 (December 1976): 6–7.

Reichmann, Felix and Tharpe, Josephine M. *Bibliographic Control of Microforms.* Westport, Connecticut: Greenwood Press, 1972.

Rice, E. Stevens. *Fiche and Reel.* Ann Arbor, Michigan: Xerox University Microfilms, 1976.

The Sourcebook of Library Technology: A Cumulated Edition of Library Technology Reports, 1965–1975. Chicago: American Library Association, 1976. (30 microfiche in pockets in a ring binder, paper copy contents page and subject index)

Spaulding, Carl M. "Kicking the Silver Habit: Confessions of a Former Addict." *American Libraries* 9 (December, 1978) 653-656; 665-669.

Spigai, Frances G. *The Invisible Medium: the State of the Art of Microform and a Guide to the Literature.* Washington: ERIC Clearinghouse on Libary and Information Sciences, 1973.

Spreitzer, Francis. "Library Microform Facilities." *Library Technology Reports* 12 (July 1976): 407–35.

Staite, Keith D. "Microforms in a College Library." *Microdoc* 15:4 1976, pp. 119–12, 122, 124–26, 128.

Studies in Micropublishing, 1853–1976, Documentary Sources. Edited by Allen B. Veaner. Westport, Connecticut: Microform Review, Inc., 1976.

Sullivan, Robert C. "Microform Developments Related to Acquisitions." *College and Research Libraries* 34 (January, 1973): 16–28.

Tannenbaum, Arthur and Sidhom, Eva. "User Environment and Attitudes in an Academic Microform Center." *Library Journal* 101 (October 15, 1976): 2139–43.

Veaner, Allen B. *The Evaluation of Micropublications: a Handbook for Librarians.* Chicago: Library Technology Program, American Library Association, 1971.

———. "Micrographics: An Eventful Forty Years—What Next?" *ALA Yearbook 1976.* Chicago: American Library Association, 1976, pp. 45–56.

———. "Micropublications." *Advances in Librarianship.* vol. 2. New York: Academic Press, 1971, pp. 165–86.

GLOSSARY*

ACETATE FILM — Safety film whose base is essentially cellulose acetate.

ADHESIVE FACE — The adhesive position on an aperture card where the tacky surface is toward the reverse side of the card, ordinarily used for mounting silver halide film.

ALPHANUMERIC — A character set that contains letters, digits, punctuation, and other machine readable records.

APERTURE — The lens opening which light passes through to create an image.

APERTURE CARD — A medium with one or several holes or apertures, that hold microfilm.

ARCHIVAL QUALITY — The ability of a processed film or print to retain its quality during prolonged use and storage. (American National Standard PH 4.8)

BACKGROUND — The non-image area of a microform or print.

BLOW-BACK — The enlargement of a microform image on a reader or readex printer.

BOOK HOLDER — A specially designed cradle to hold a book open (especially bound books) while it is photographed.

CARD-TO-CARD PRINTER — Duplicating equipment that creates, by contact printing, duplicate card-mounted microforms.

CHARACTER TRANSFER RATE — The speed of transfer when characters are relayed from maganetic tape to computer, computers to microform, etc.

COM   Computer Output Microform is filmed data produced on a recorder from computer records, with film substituting for the traditional paper printouts.

CONTACT PRINTING   Reproduction achieved by bringing unexposed film stock into direct contact with the master copy.

CONTRAST   The difference between high and low brightness or density of a photograph. A photograph has high contrast when the difference between minimum and maximum density is large.

COPY   A duplication of an original document, or the process of making a duplication.

CORE   The center of a spool, cartridge, cassette or reel.

DEFINITION   That quality of a photo image concerned with clarity or sharpness of detail.

DENSITOMETER   An instrument for measuring optical density. The two basic types are transmission (to measure opacity) and reflection (used to measure amount of light reflected by a surface).

DENSITY   The light absorbing qualify of a photographic image, usually expressed as the common logarithm of the ratio of the amount of light striking the image. Several specific types of density values for a photograph may be expressed but diffuse transmission density is of greatest value in the case of microfilm, and diffuse reflection density is generally of interest for prints.

DIAMETERS   Reduction, enlargement, or magnification. A measure of the number of times a given linear dimension of an object is reduced or enlarged by an optical system.

DIAZO MATERIAL   Film or paper sensitized with diazonium salts. Such film, when exposed to blue to ultraviolet light, forms an image. Diazo film ordinarily is non-reversible. A positive image will produce a positive image; a negative image produces a negative image.

DIRECT IMAGE FILM   Film that produces a negative from a negative or a positive from a positive.

DIRECT POSITIVE   A positive image which is made from another positive without using a negative intermediary. Negatives also can be produced directly from other negatives.

DISTRIBUTION COPIES   Microform prints run from camera-generated originals or intermediates, prepared for distribution to users.

DRY SILVER   Film which is non-gelatin and is developed with a heating process.

DUPLICATE   A copy made usually with contact printing, or (verb) the making of duplicate copies.

ELECTRONIC BEAM RECORDER   A COM unit which generates images directly onto EBR microfilm.

EMULSION   The light sensitive coating on microfilm usually containing silver salts and other chemicals suspended in gelatin.

ENLARGER-PRINTER   A machine that projects enlarged images from microform.

EXPOSURE   (1) The act of exposing a light-sensitive material to a light source.
(2) A section of a film containing an individual frame or image, as in a roll containing six exposures.
(3) Exposure time; i.e., the time during which a light sensitive surface is exposed to a light source.
(4) The product of light intensity and the time during which it acts on photosensitive material.

FACSIMILE   An exact reproduction of an original document.

FILM   A sheet or strip of transparent plastic which is treated with a light-sensitive emulsion.

FILM JACKETS   Plastic envelopes with slots to carry individual frames of film.

FILM, MASTER   Film produced during the first filming of a document.

FILM, ORTHOCHROMATIC   Film which has an emulsion that is sensitive to ultraviolet, violet, blue, green radiation. Red subjects photographed with orthochromatic film are rendered dark on prints.

FILM, PANCHROMATIC   A black and white film with an emulsion that is sensitive to ultraviolet, violet, blue, green, and red radiation.

FILM PRINT   A contact copy reproduced from master film.

FILM REVERSAL   Film that is processed to produce a positive image instead of a negative one.

FILM ROLL   Film wound on a spool, usually 100 or 200 feet in length.

FINDER LIGHT   A light beam projected from some cameras to show the outline of the photographic field at a particular reduction ratio. This field is sometimes further delineated by reticular lines and other guide marks.

FLATS   Pieces of smooth, flat optical glass designed to hold microforms in place for reading.

FOCUS   The plane in which rays of light reflected from a surface converge to form the sharpest possible image of the original after passing through the several parts of a lens, or the process of adjusting the relative positions of the lens and film to obtain the sharpest possible image.

FRAME   The area of film exposed to light through the camera optical system during one exposure, regardless of whether or not the area is filled by the document image.

GENERATION   A way of measuring the successive number of copies made from original material. An original picture is called first generation. Reproductions made from the original are called second generation, third generation, etc.

HALIDE   A light sensitive compound of chlorine, iodine, bromine or fluorine.

HARD COPY   Popular name for non-microform copy, or copy that can be read without magnification.

HYPO   Sodium or ammonium thiosulfate used in fixing baths to remove unexposed silver halides from silver emulsion film; also applied to the complete fixing bath, which may contain other chemicals.

IMAGE   (1) A reproduction of an object, produced by light rays.
(2) A photographic reproduction of an object on film.

INTERMEDIATE   A reproducible, which may be microfilm, made from the original document. Used to make additional copies.

KALFAX   An emulsion sensitive to ultraviolet light, coated with mylar base, and processed with heat.

LEADER   A strip of blank film at the beginning of a roll which is used for threading a camera, projector or processor.

LENS   One or more glass sections specially ground for directing light rays by refraction to form an image.

MAGNIFICATION   The ratio of an object viewed through an optical instrument to the size of the same object viewed by the naked eye. Extent of magnification is ordinarily given in diameters or times, e.g., 24×.

MASTER FILM   Any film, but generally a negative, used solely for making copies as opposed to film used in readers.

MICROCOPY   A copy made with photography which is too small to be read with the naked eye.

MICROFICHE   Sheet film that contains several rows of micro-images.

MICROFILM   Fine-grain, fine resolution photographic film carrying or designed to carry photographic images greatly reduced in size and usually too small to be read with the unaided eye.

MICROFORM   A generic term for any format or film or paper carrying microimages.

MICROGRAPHICS   An industry which reduces information sources to microform.

MICROIMAGE   A source of information too small to be read with the unaided eye.

MICRO-OPAQUE (MICROCARD)   A sheet of opaque material containing microimages.

MICROPHOTOGRAPH   A photograph so small as to require magnification for reading.

MICROPRINT   A micro-opaque developed by the Readex Microprint Company.

MICROPUBLISHING   Marketing new or reformatted information in microform to the public.

NEGATIVE   A microfilm or microfilm image in which the tonal values are reversed from those in the original; light areas are recorded as dark, and dark areas as light.

ORIGINAL   The object from which copies are produced.

PANCHROMATIC   An emulsion that is sensitive to all visible colors.

PHOTOSENSITIVE   A condition of sensitivity to the action of visible light.

POLARITY   A condition of change or retention of the dark to light relationship of an image. Creating a second generation positive from a first generation negative is a polarity change.

POSITIVE   A microfilm or microfilm image in which the tonal values are the same as in the original; light areas are recorded as light, dark areas as dark.

PRINT   A reproduction on film or paper.

PRINTER   Equipment that produces prints. Card-to-card printers duplicate aperture cards in contact printing; roll-to-roll printers create duplicate roll film; enlarger-printers create enlarged prints.

PROCESSING   The chemical or physical treatment of exposed photographic material to make visible the latent image; i.e., a series of steps consisting of developing, fixing, washing, and drying.

RAW STOCK   Sensitized material which has not been exposed or processed.

READER   A self-contained device combining a projector and screen used for viewing enlarged microimages with the naked eye.

READER-PRINTER   Equipment that combines the features of a reader and an enlarger-printer.

REDUCTION RATIO   The ratio of a linear dimension of the original document to the corresponding dimension of the image on the microfilm, expressed as 14:1, 24:1, or 14×, 24× etc.

REEL   A flanged holder for film, usually for processed film (as opposed to a spool for unprocessed film).

RESIDUAL HYPO   Sodium or ammonium thiosulfate remaining in film or paper after washing. Since residual hypo has a deleterious effect and reduces film life, careful control must be maintained in processing to ensure that permissible limits are not exceeded.

RESOLVING POWER   The degree to which a lens is able to produce, or a film emulusion to record, fine detail in a micro-image, expressed as the number of lines per millimeter discernible in the image.

SILVER HALIDE   A compound of silver and any one of the following elements (Hologens): Chlorine, bromine, iodine, fluorine.

SPLICE   A joint made by cementing or welding (heat splicing) together two pieces of film or paper so they will function as a single piece when passing through a camera, processing machine, projector, or other apparatus. In cemented splices, known as lap splices, one piece overlaps the other. Most welds are called butt splices because the two pieces are butted together without any overlap; some butt splices also use tape.

TARGET   (1) A document or chart containing identification information, coding or test charts.
    (2) An aid to technical or bibliographical control which is photographed on the film preceding or following the document proper.

ULTRAFICHE   Microfiche having a reduction ratio in excess of 90×.

VESICULAR FILM   Film having a light sensitive element suspended in a plastic layer that when exposed creates stains.

*The National Micrographics Association's *Glossary of Micrographics* has been followed as closely as possible in the compilation of this glossary.

Index

173